Drawing with Confidence

Venice, 1975. Felt pen.

Drawing with Confidence

James R. Turner

VENICE

VNR VAN NOSTRAND REINHOLD COMPANY
NEW YORK   CINCINNATI   TORONTO   LONDON   MELBOURNE

Printed in the United States of America
Designed by Loudan Enterprises
All art by the author unless otherwise indicated

Published by Van Nostrand Reinhold Company Inc.
135 West 50th Street
New York, New York 10020

Van Nostrand Reinhold
480 La Trobe Street
Melbourne, Victoria 3000, Australia

Macmillan of Canada
Division of Gage Publishing Limited
164 Commander Boulevard
Agincourt, Ontario M1S 3C7, Canada

16 15 14 13 12 11 10 9 8 7 6 5 4 3 2 1
Library of Congress Cataloging in Publication Data
Turner, James R.
   Drawing with confidence.
   Includes index.
   1. Drawing—Technique.   I. Title.
NC730.T87   1984   741.2   82-25929
ISBN 0-442-28286-9

Contents

*Go
get
yourself
an
ordinary
pencil.*

*Now—
draw
some
lines
on
this
page,*

*sort
of
over
there
somewhere.*

*Good.
Very good.*

Part II

Developing Confidence

Introduction

Cape Cod, 1979. Pencil.

Formal principles of drawing are a great comfort to the teacher but of little use to the student. They are important, but I learned them long after I learned how to draw. A child's first drawings arise from feelings and not principles. In time, we shall deal with principles, but first let's deal with drawing.

One of the first essentials, no matter how much of a beginner you are, is to gain confidence in yourself. The road to confidence is an interesting study in itself, and there are perhaps as many roads as there are people. You must not be concerned with the route you take so much as with the fact that you do, sooner or later, arrive. For example, in drawing tracing is an acceptable road. So trace, copy, fudge, use others and their work. We all do it all the time. There is nothing that we do that is not in some way repetition. But you do need to consider the positive spirit of the imitation—to learn with confidence. To instill confidence then is the major goal of this book. With confidence you can move mountains—or at least draw them so moved.

This book, or I would like to say this beginning, is like a musical scale. Musical scales and concertos are related, but in a way that cannot predict the concerto's potential beauty. And so it is with drawing. Who knows what beauty may appear on a sheet of paper? I like to compare drawing to good music, even good literature and crafts, because I believe it helps to un-derstand and appreciate its value. You as an artist, designer, or illustrator can take great pride in the medium with which you communicate—drawing.

Certainly there are varying degrees of accomplishment. The individual level of achievement is one reality, but choosing to do your best is another. You can learn to draw, of

Wheelbarrow, 1982. Felt pen.

that you can be sure. Henry Millon, MIT professor and director of the American Academy in Rome, once remarked, "Most of us are not interested in greatness, just in common, ordinary, everyday achievement."

The word *gifted* is often used in relation to artists. Many famous psychiatrists, such as Freud and Jung, believed that a person may have an artistic inclination, or gift. But even if this belief is true, such a gift represents an almost immeasurable fraction compared to what can be achieved through hard work and practice.

As a part of these preliminaries it is appropriate to include a few other important elements. First, learning to draw is a dynamic and exciting experience that can always use new and fresh approaches. We are rapidly becoming a more visually oriented society. We take in great quantities of professional graphic communication every day. Even small towns have their artists, galleries, and commercial illustrators and designers. It is more and more common to find drawing-oriented people playing important roles in society. Commercial artists, architects, landscape architects, engineers, city planners, industrial and interior designers, and even many scientists, mathematicians, and archaeologists are communicating in the language of drawings and diagrams. I feel that a new, practical approach to drawing is timely and relevant.

The second important point is the relationship of drawing and psychology. Much lies between the lines of any book; as we all know from experience, much goes unsaid. But the truth is that learning to draw is a rather miraculous phenomenon. You bring to this new experience all the nuances of your personality. Your infinitely complex self constantly interprets what you learn in its own way. You are quite unique, and your drawings will be unique—unlike anyone else's. There is no single method of developing confidence in drawing. Creative insight exists, to be sure, but of necessity it must remain between the lines.

A third point has to do with what I call "making room." We are not partial people; we are whole people. We are whole in the sense that our minds and our lives are not empty. We may have some overdrawn or stale accounts, but vacancies are not the mind's forte. What the mind cannot fill with reality it will fill with illusion and vice versa. Even in our earliest days we were whole. However, as psychoanalyst June Singer has stated, we have a great capacity to make room for new mental and physical interests. The mind can and does continuously take in and store information. To our dismay, it can also hide this information—at times even the name of a dear friend may be momentarily lost. This allocation capacity allows you to make room. Learning to draw requires this sort of warehouse activity of the mind. Make room for the new. Store some of the not-so-needed. Air out a guest room.

And finally, this is a "how to" and "why to" book. In *The Zen of Seeing*, Frederick Franc deals with the core of learning to draw—seeing. Franc's message is more than a passing note. To learn to draw, you must learn to see. Seeing extends worlds beyond technique, beyond thinking, to a harmony of hand and feeling relationships. How clearly I remember during an around-the-world trip how even to

blink was bothersome; so happy were my eyes that I know seeing is the lifeblood of drawing.

Within all of us there is an artist. For you to become acquainted with that artist within, begin now to swell your senses and your confidence: the fragrances, the melodies, the wet grass, the birds scratching, the spirit in stones, the bittersweet taste of your own perspiration, and the seeing—the seeing of the ten thousand details even in a single leaf.

Singapore harbor, 1976. Chinese pen.

Embarcadero, 1976. Felt pen.

1. To Start With

Drawing involves practice. If you practice, you will improve. Practice is essentially the secret of drawing. And it is always more fun to begin a new thing knowing the secret of its success.

When I first began teaching people to draw, I had to decide what would be the most important and appropriate starting point. I read dozens of books on drawing. Most began with all the paraphernalia the student needed to buy. Many started with the great masters and their masterpieces. Still others began with the work of the author. And so on. Through every book, however, ran a common theme: *practice!* Even books by the most sophisticated practitioners or world-renowned artists would soon state: Practice regularly and often.

So how do you practice? And provided you have decided to do so, with what do you start?

To learn to draw you must begin. Chicken scratches are a natural beginning. I would encourage you to draw *on* anything, *with* anything. A good place to begin is right here, in the margins. I've done some of my best scratches in my books.

Getting to know how to use the pencil can be compared to any craftsman's initial contact with his or her tools. The bricklayer's trowel, the

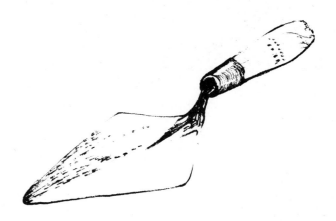

sculptor's chisel, the welder's torch, or the barber's scissors are all extensions of the special skills they represent. This skill matures in proportion to the intimate relationship and harmony the craftsman shares with the tools.

   Do things with your pencils. Put them behind your ears. Carry them around in your hand. Sharpen them with a pocketknife or razor blade just to learn how. Think of them, and imagine all that they have been through. I have hundreds of old pencils. It is nice having them around. Take a close look at your pencil for a moment. It is really a rather marvelous and ancient tool, symbolic of one of man's quantum leaps—learning to write, which, by the way, came long after we learned to draw.

I like to begin with the square or rectangle as a point of departure for creative chicken scratching. Using a soft pencil, create exercises that simply familiarize you with the pencil.

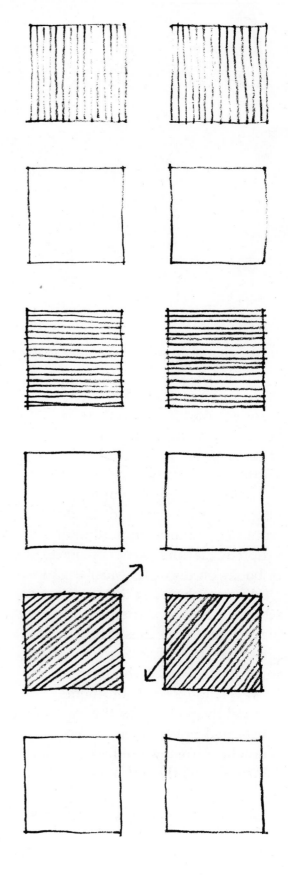

Getting familiar with
the pencil is a primary goal
of these scratches.

Just drawing little boxes within which to
create doodles is a good exercise. Get
yourself a notebook or pad (Courage!)
and start like this

you may have an inclination toward certain objects or symbols.
It is well known that doodles play a multiple role in our
lives— relieving anxiety, releasing aggressions and sexual tensions,
and allowing us to daydream with a modicum of usefulness.

Try out a few on
your imagination.

What you want the doodling exercises to do for you is, first, to get you intimately in tune with the tool. It is important to know its subtleties. Second, the exercises should give you control over the kinds of strokes, how dark, how close together, how many, how few, and how fast you can manage them. Third, you want to stir your creative imagination, get yourself thinking about, searching for, and discovering the many variations that are possible. And fourth, you want these exercises to refresh you and prepare you to go on to more involved and larger drawings.

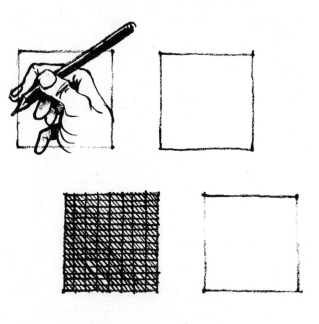

Whenever, if ever, you don't like a certain stroke or another, that's the time to make the exercises pay off. I often hear, for example, "I can't draw a straight line." Well its not going to happen overnight, but if you will fill a few pages of your notebook with nothing but straight lines, you will see marked improvement.

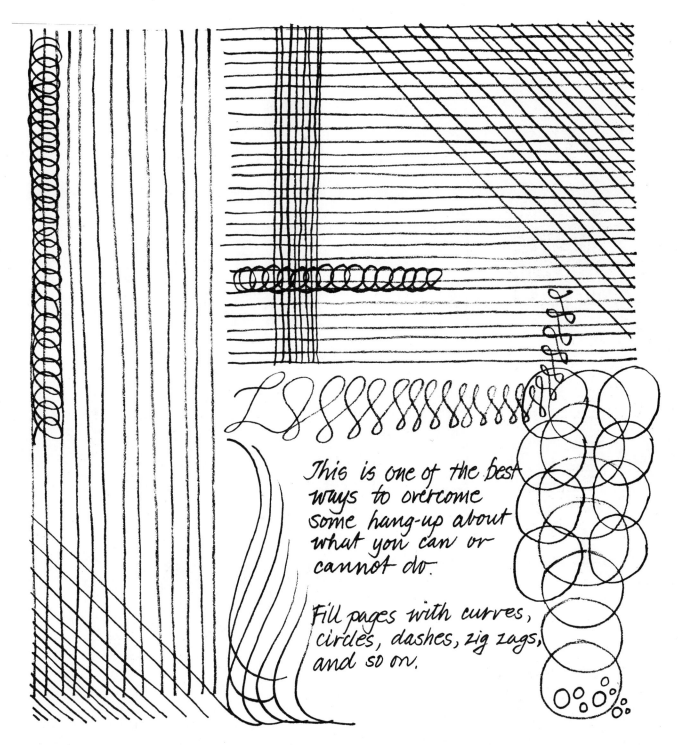

This is one of the best ways to overcome some hang-up about what you can or cannot do.

Fill pages with curves, circles, dashes, zig zags, and so on.

I must point out here that your individuality is in no way threatened by the discipline required to fill a one-inch square. No, quite the contrary. Creativity and individuality are not governed by the size of a square. To think of and execute a pattern in a small square with imagination and skill can be as involved as producing a ten-foot canvas.

patterns and inventions

Uneven strokes

continuous lines

Finally, on the subject of warming up, there are some rather specific exercises that you might try just to familiarize yourself with the range of things the pencil can achieve.

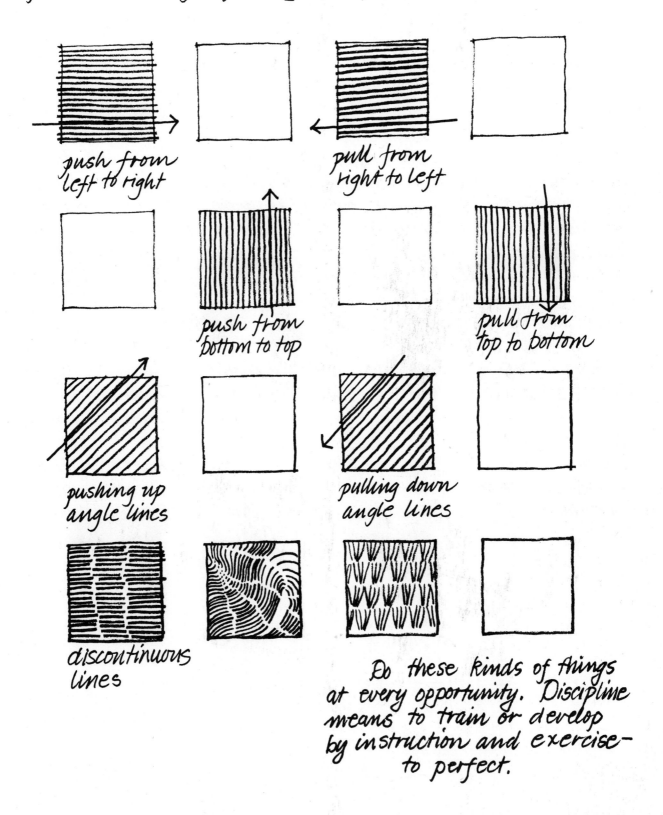

push from
left to right

pull from
right to left

push from
bottom to top

pull from
top to bottom

pushing up
angle lines

pulling down
angle lines

discontinuous
lines

Do these kinds of things at every opportunity. Discipline means to train or develop by instruction and exercise— to perfect.

| an unusual view of a detail | Like lipstick | Was once a part of a tree | It communi-cates like a copper wire |

Try this warm-up technique. Each day choose a word to illustrate. Pick anything you like, then brainstorm little doodles that have something to do with the person, place, or thing you've chosen. Above I picked the PENCIL and did four literal squares that have something to do with the pencil.

Here are some words to get you started:

Tires	Tape	Ruler	Sheep	Clouds	Comb	Cap
Fork	Ticket	Razor	Ring	Pelican	Rooster	Bottle
Keys	Shoe	Twezers	Wrench	Cradle	Board	Anthill
Canary	Taxes	Toad	Film	Steer	Wart	Muff
Dragon	Denver	Dwarf	Clamp	Fair	Heart	Zebra
Purse	Detour	Pin	Parkway	Toothpaste	Trumpet	Kite
Calendar	Nail	Spiral	Highrise	Shovel	Flower	Jar

Doodling provides several other valuable services. It requires no great commitment and thereby serves as a transition to other drawing challenges. It lets you explore and search for techniques to represent things such as leaves and rocks. It helps you to think and to compare solutions to problems. So scratch and see what happens.

Siena roofs, 1975. Brown felt pen.

2. Strokes

Line drawing is essentially drawing with fairly well-defined strokes. I mention line drawing first because for everyone except a few specialized artists, the line is the core of communication. In one of Van Gogh's famous letters to his brother Theo he said, ". . . my pencil drawings are the backbone of my paintings." Many of the most famous artists relied on line drawings to generate ideas and display preliminary plans for future commissions. Sometimes the lines were accomplished with chalk or ink and even neutral colors of paint. Many other things have been employed, such as charcoal, oil pastels, and so on. Of course, architects, draftsmen, engineers, interior designers, commercial artists, illustrators, engravers, and a great number of others must depend on line drawings for their day-to-day work.

Before going into the techniques of line drawing, consider the two words *a* and *the*. If you think about it for a moment, you will be able to see what I'm driving at: *a* means one of many (*a* girl, *a* bike, etc.); *the* means unique, matchless (*the* Abe Lincoln, *the* Buddha, etc.). The point is that you can learn *a* way of doing something or *the* way of doing it. From this book, you will learn *a* way of drawing—not *the* way. This is an important distinction, one you should keep in mind as you progress.

Now let's continue with the value of line drawings versus other types of drawings. Probably one of the most important reasons to develop your skills with lines is that they are quick. Perhaps this is a reflection of our society. Being able to communicate quickly has obvious advantages. Concepts can be rapidly symbolized; ideas can go back and forth; plans can be made and minor adjustments or major changes can be accommodated.

Our visual perceivers (the ways we see) have been trained to understand the line. This is an ancient characteristic. People have a great historical association with lines. They can be moved to reverence, to fear, and to laughter in large part through their exposure to lines—the lines that comprise symbols, which in turn trigger the deeper-seated responses. Of all the ways to draw, lines are the most easily understood.

In the last fifty years, there has been a sort of quiet revolution in the sharing of information. Everyone wants a copy. The printing and duplicating segments of industry have expanded tremendously. Once again, line drawing has been the most suit-

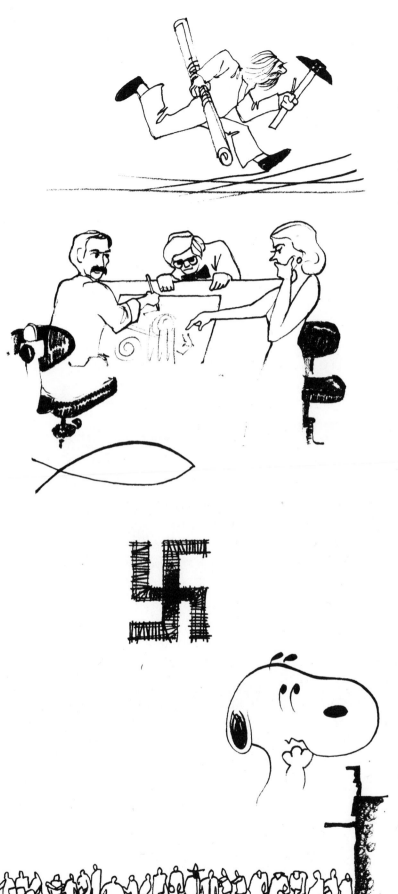

able technique. They can be easily duplicated.

Tone drawing is essentially drawing variations of "weight." This is accomplished by relatively even but undefined strokes.

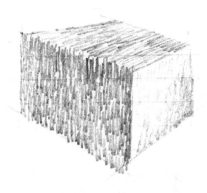

Tone drawing is really nothing more than a collection of lines, but with an important difference. Notice that the edges are created by the planes of the sides. With a line drawing the planes would be created by the lines or edges themselves.

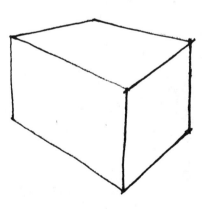

Tone drawing is also called shading. It is an excellent way to draw because it can express surfaces so well. Shading is the principal way to paint. You will notice that paintings use colors in varying shades to achieve their effect. Naturally a drawing done only with tones would take more time to complete.

What proves to be most useful is a combination of the two extremes. Mixing the two allows you to take full advantage of each.

Doing an exposé on technique has a positive effect on confidence. If you haven't thought of it before now, more than likely there was a fair amount of hocus-pocus surrounding your understanding of drawing. I know we are still some distance from "drawing confidence," but if we can systematically chop away at some of the tricks, we'll get there. So here is what we know about drawing strokes: there are fundamentally only two possibilities—lines and tones. There are endless variations on these two strokes. And, if this helps, there is actually only one way to draw: with a deliberate and practiced line. All drawings are made with lines. It is as

simple as that. Master the line, and much of what's left involves adapting the line to your favor.

In texts by the better drawing experts, Theodore Kautzky and Frank Rines, for example, much time is devoted to the subject of line control, often a complete chapter. I reiterate its value and give you this final word: practice, copy others, trace, invent, create patterns and overlapping elements. They need not be literal, but if it helps, think of surfaces and things. Try to approximate them with different strokes. Try things like wood grain, long hair, sandpaper, quilts, marbles, fishing poles, watermelons, figs, and cauliflowers.

As we expose the tricks that hold drawings together, and as you practice and become proficient at arranging these tricks, please try to keep this in mind: behind and beyond all the lines is the magic and mystery of the well-done whole sketch. All of its illusory film can never be removed. And it shouldn't be. Remember early experiences, remember drawings that you really liked. Even though you will come to know much about how they are done, don't be above responding to great or favorite drawings in a less academic way.

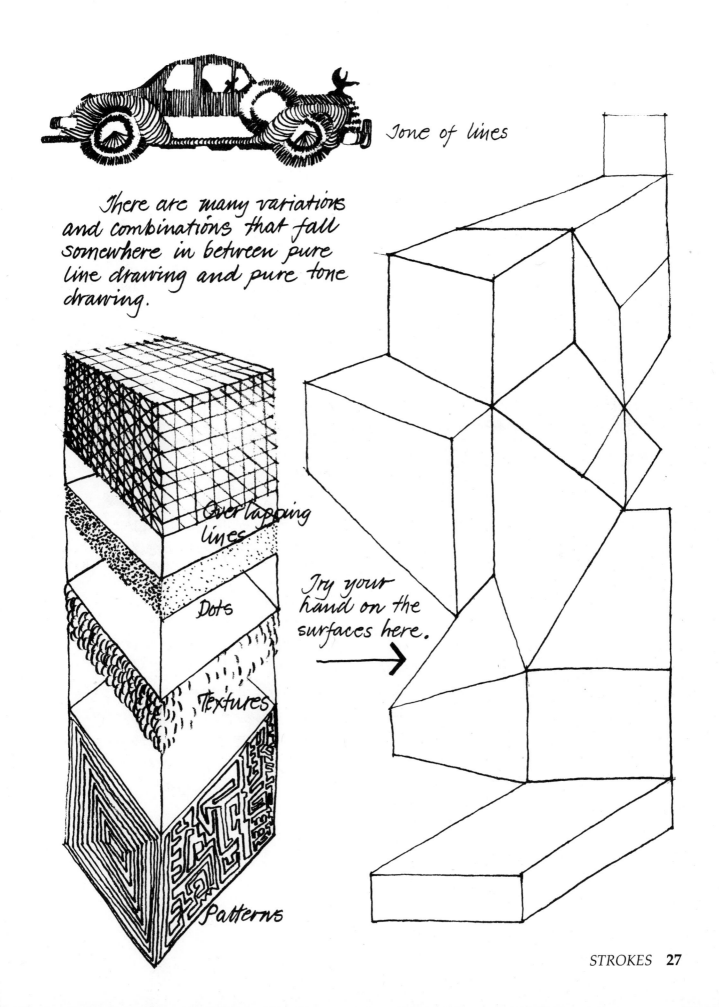

Tone of lines

There are many variations and combinations that fall somewhere in between pure line drawing and pure tone drawing.

Overlapping lines

Dots

Textures

Patterns

Try your hand on the surfaces here.

Here are a few suggestions that should aid in developing your skill with various strokes. First you want to be comfortable, allowing yourself the room and space around you that you need.

Next, hold the pencil naturally. If your knuckles are turning white or you are cramped, you're not going to last long.

Relax your hold on the pencil.

You can steady your drawing hand by placing your little finger down like a brace. Also you can rest the heel of your hand on the page and pull inward or push outward with your thumb and forefinger while in this position.

Learn what various points can do.

A fine, new, sharp point can make a crisp, clean line.

A bevel, flat point can make a fat stroke or a knifelike cut.

A nicely rounded point can be used in different ways depending on your needs. I will usually use a nicely rounded point. The best solution, however, is to have several sharpened pencils around, with a good variety of points from which to choose.

Ram Bagh, Jaipur, 1976. Ball-point pen.

Making strokes just for fun and practice will lead to more accomplished pieces. In the drawing done at the beautiful Ram Bagh Palace in Jaipur, India, I originally intended to express only the old wicker chairs in the foreground, but one stroke led to another until I had a much more interesting sketch.

Casa Frollo, 1976. Red felt pen. (Courtesy of Susan L. Turner)

3. Supplies

If you don't already have a stock of your own supplies, let me give you a list that will get you started.

First, the *pencil*. Several different media have been used so far in this book. You are encouraged to try any tool you like, but the pencil is our foundation.

My preference is the Eagle Draughting · 314.

Have you ever noticed that when you are sharpening your pencil, the lead sometimes keeps breaking?

Usually this indicates that the pencil has been dropped. When a pencil falls on a hard surface, the lead will break into small segments inside the wood. Treating your tools with respect and consideration will help you establish a rapport with them.

The supplies needed to draw with pen and ink are few, simple, and easy to acquire. The many ink drawings you see in this book attest to my faith in this medium.

I have several favorite pens, which you are encouraged again to experiment with. Many of the drawings throughout this book were done with either a ball-point pen or one of the various hard-tipped felt pens. With the ball-point, everything is dependent upon line control, but with felt pens you can get into a good bit of shading. Keep those old ones that are almost dry—that's when you can really achieve some nice effects.

Many teachers/authors make a big to-do about the number and kinds of pencils you should have. For the beginner I feel that one or maybe two are sufficient.

Another excellent drawing tool is the Ebony # 6325 made by Eberhard Faber.

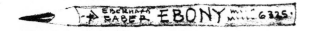

Notice that if you sharpen the pencil on the end opposite the number, you always have a record of what you are using. This is especially important with colored pencils or the more expensive draughting (drafting) pencils. I won't go into all the possibilities here except to say that, again, the softer pencils (B, 2B, 4B, etc.) are your best choices for now.

But lets use the KISS method (Keep it simple stupid) almost anything will do - even the common #1 pencil.

I don't recommend the use of ink pens until some drawing confidence is achieved. It will most likely overtake the other techniques in your repertoire soon enough. As you gain experience, however, or as the opportunity presents itself, there are several types of ink pens to try.

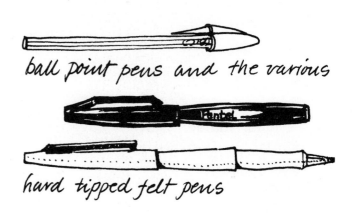

ball point pens and the various

hard tipped felt pens

Next, *paper*. Paper is somewhat of a mystery to me because I have seen many outstanding drawings done on very modest paper. My recommendation is that you shop around for a smooth, white, cheap paper, either bound or loose-leaf. When you get your first drawing commission, you can rush out and get that expensive bristol board or whatever. For now, let's stick to smooth, white, and cheap. Cheap paper also has the added advantage of not intimidating you as much. If you are going to harbor any reservations about freely stroking a piece of paper because of its quality or its price, you will be establishing an unnecessary barrier between yourself and the drawing confidence you need.

The easiest and most precise are the KOH·I·NOOR rapidograph or the STAEDTLER drafting pens. These work like fountain pens and the stroke can vary only if you change the size of the pen's point.

These pens are very expensive and they take time to master, but almost nothing can equal the precision and regularity you can expect from them.

Of course you can't get by without mentioning the old dip type speedball pens. Probably nothing can exhibit such character of line as one of these old veterans.

The ordinary fountain pen such as the cheap "no-nonsense" pens with fat points are the favorite of many - they are hard to top for price and convenience.

Turner '73

Self-portrait with a a favorite old pen.

Use paper freely, as a means to an end. The paper used in a single day by fast-food chains is more than that used by artists since the invention of paper. Scavenge, draw on anything—brown envelopes, paper bags, napkins, tablecloths, whatever is handy. Draw on the backs of used paper. Do not, however, draw on the backs of your own or others' drawings unless you are particularly desperate. This is a cardinal rule, unless you have no other choice.

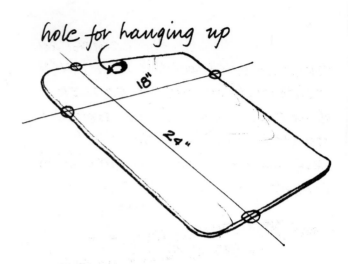

hole for hanging up

18"

24"

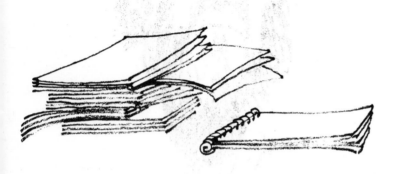

The next item that I find handy is a *drawing board*. If you work only at your desk and/or you have a large drawing pad with a stiff back, you may get by without a drawing board. However, my experience has been that a small drawing board is needed. It can be made of any material available. Mine is an old-fashioned lapboard-type made from ¼-inch plywood, sanded and varnished. But as I said, it can be made or purchased. You can also buy one with built-in clips and a carrying handle.

Whenever you're drawing, whatever you're drawing on, try to cushion it. By this I mean that you should have several layers of paper between the pencil point and the surface upon which the paper is placed. The reason for this is unique to the pencil. A pencil depends on pressure to make a visible mark. The small amount of bounce you get by cushioning the surface with several sheets of paper gives the pencil its special style. Inks and color media do not share this more subtle quality. By varying the pressure on the pencil you vary the line. Without a cushion you may be struggling against the drawing surface, its grain, its texture, etc.

paper

drawing surface

Clips and big rubber bands are good to have along for those windy days.

I use a cotton rag to minimize the smudges. Sometimes I place it under the heel of my hand to avoid sweating on the paper.

A *sharpening device* is another good thing to have along in the field and, of course, is a must in the studio. There is no substitute, as far as I'm concerned, for a good mechanical pencil sharpener, but it isn't always the most practical thing to have in your bag. There are other hand-held devices that can do a tolerable job, and you shouldn't be above using a pocketknife or a razor blade. Electric sharpeners are a real luxury. I wouldn't turn one down if it were offered.

At this point let me remind you that one of the important things to remember is neatness. When you've finished, and sometimes during your work, stop and clean up. Keep those smudges and muddy fingerprints to a minimum.

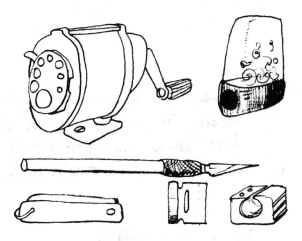

Some rather finicky illustrators insist on using the mechanical pencil with softer leads and a sanding block or fingernail file to shape the point. It sounds like a clean, practical system. I hope it does not get in the way of good, down-to-earth drawing.

Erasers should be used sparingly if at all. You can use an eraser, but don't let it become a crutch. You will be learning later how to use "preliminary lines," how to look at things and "see" them, and how to plan ahead. Get a soft graphite eraser, but start now to avoid eraser mentality: "Only the correct things can stay on my paper." I've witnessed many novices making a cautious stroke, then erasing it and doing it again until they give up in frustration, eat a hole in the paper, or, now and then, finally get it "right."

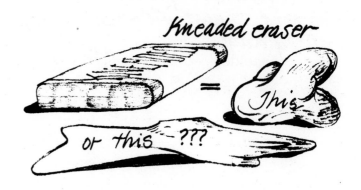

Kneaded eraser — *This*

or this — ???

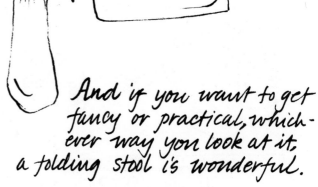

Graphite eraser:

soft, usually white, not to be confused with similar ink erasers. Ink erasers are hard and can easily tear the paper fiber.

Your day-to-day supplies might also include a carrying case, a sturdy little bag or box. It need be only the length of a pencil.

A graphite eraser is soft and usually white. It is not to be confused with similar ink erasers, which are hard and can easily tear the paper fiber.

And if you want to get fancy or practical, whichever way you look at it, a folding stool is wonderful.

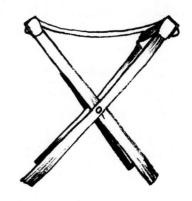

A kneaded eraser is a more specialized item, and you can give it a try if you are so inclined. It is meant to be molded like clay or dough, hence kneaded. It is used to pick up and lighten the drawing, not to remove it. It works best when it is pulled and stretched and warmed by your hands.

a can of spray matte fixative. This spray protects from smudges and moisture.

In order to put finishing touches on your work you can keep the following items at the studio:

a good sharp mat knife

an 18" or longer cutting edge

a flexible metal edge works well

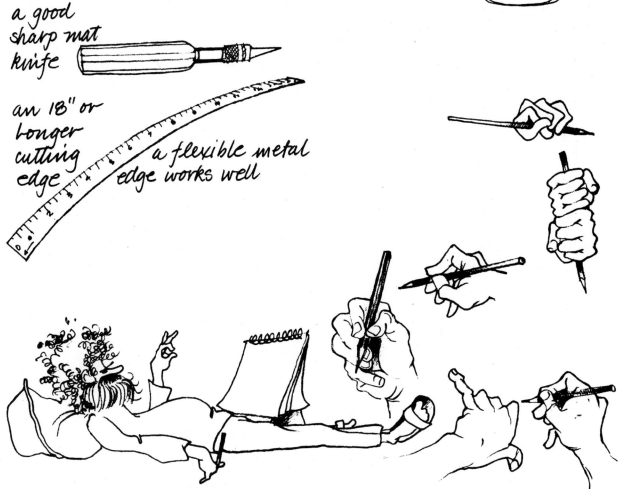

Keeping a pad or blotter close to the telephone in both the home and the studio is a good idea because all sorts of good scratches can appear quite independent of your telephone conversations or while waiting for your party to answer.

In the squares below begin doodling with a selection of the supplies you've now acquired.

Before going further into any more particular drawing techniques, here is an important point. You can already draw. That's correct. You can already draw. Think about the drawings that you did when you were a child. Your teachers or parents had only to give you a pad and a few crayons and off you'd go. It was fantastic. Remember also how proud and excited you were about these drawings? Look at the work of your own or others' small children. It is fresh, unique, and spontaneous. Today you may not be too proud of those old yellowed drawings. Indeed you may not even have any of them left. But if you would consider the free and carefree mind and hand that produced them, you would have to agree that they have significance and worth. By the way, many children's drawings are in museums and private collections, and many collectors are attracted to the so-called primitives because these paintings have maintained a childlike freshness.

Somewhere between the ages of eight and twelve, at least in our present society, these drawings are put aside. Today they are being reconsidered. One technique used in psychology is to have people express themselves through drawings. Drawings with titles such as *My Neighborhood* or *My Favorite Place* are very revealing.

The point is this: you can draw even if it is as a child. Use it to your advantage. Draw with abandon. Draw anything. No size and no source is sacred. Draw. That is what counts. The preceding exercises and the more formal work that we are about to begin are all secondary to this important point—you can draw. These drawings are good, and they can be downright engaging works of creativity. So, go to it.

".... The whole technical power of painting depends on our recovery of what may be called the INNOCENCE OF THE EYE; That is to say, of a sort of childish perception of these flat stains of colour, merely as such, without consciousness of what they signify, as a blind man would see them if suddenly gifted with sight.... Strive, therefore, first of all to convince yourself of this great fact about sight. This, in your hand, which you know by experience and touch to be a book, is to your eye nothing but a patch of white, variously gradated and spotted."

Ruskin, Elements of Drawing 1857

Von Odenwald. Combat, 1970. Pencil, 3" x 5".
Sports, 1971. Ball-point, 3" x 5".
Adventure, 1971. Pencil, 3" x 5".
(Courtesy of the artist, age 7)

4. The Side View

Now, you could start off by drawing almost anything, but I like to use the ordinary things of our everyday environment. These things are accessible, available, and familiar. Primarily they are cars, trees, buildings, land, sky, water, and people. Although there are ten thousand things from which you could choose, to me, these are the essentials. Furthermore, learning to draw one thing is like eating a peanut; you can hardly stop with just one. The things you learn about drawing a car, for example, will apply to a boat, an airplane, or a herd of wheelbarrows.

As you begin to look at cars, *proportion* will be your first concern. Proportion is the relative height to width of an object. Let's begin with the front of a typical small car. From the front, the average car will have a proportion of approximately 5 to 6 or 2½ to 3. It doesn't make any difference what the units are. They are relative to one another—5 units high to 6 units wide.

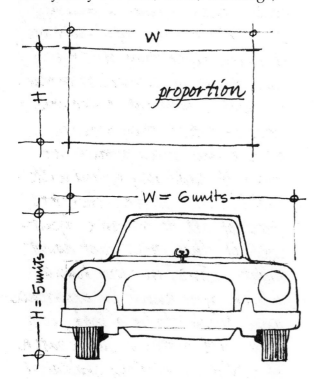

This is an excellent starting point: draw the basic H-TO-W relationship of things around you. Don't be concerned with shape.

one unit equals one unit

Caroline Durieux. Art Class, 1939. (Courtesy of the artist)

There is no particularly secret way of getting at proportion. Proportion is the relative height to width of any object or space. You can measure it visually with your outstretched hand, or, with practice and some hard *seeing*, proportion will make itself known to you.

If you are looking at the front view of a car, with your drawing paper, board, pencil, etc. in position, you are probably already saying, "what is he talking about?"

Relax - you see proportion is relative height to width.

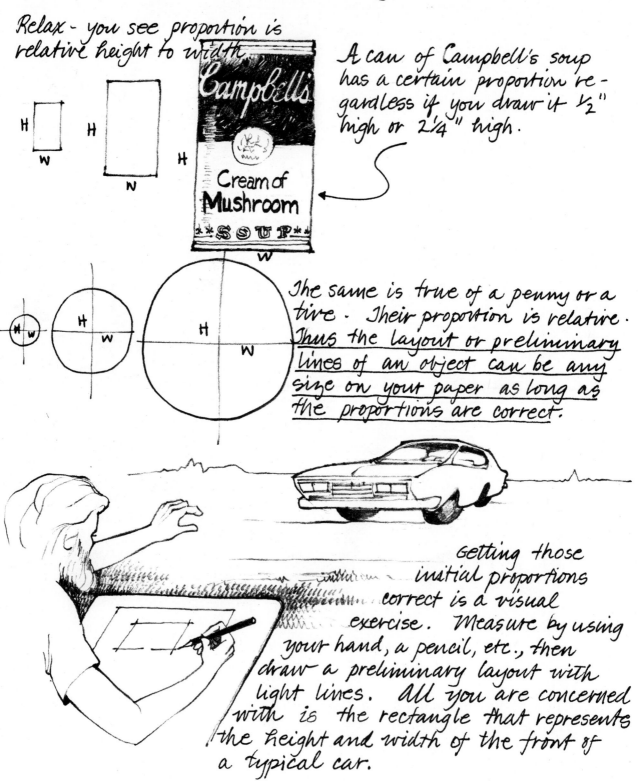

A can of Campbell's soup has a certain proportion re- gardless if you draw it ½" high or 2¼" high.

The same is true of a penny or a tire. Their proportion is relative. Thus the layout or preliminary lines of an object can be any size on your paper as long as the proportions are correct.

Getting those initial proportions correct is a visual exercise. Measure by using your hand, a pencil, etc., then draw a preliminary layout with light lines. All you are concerned with is the rectangle that represents the height and width of the front of a typical car.

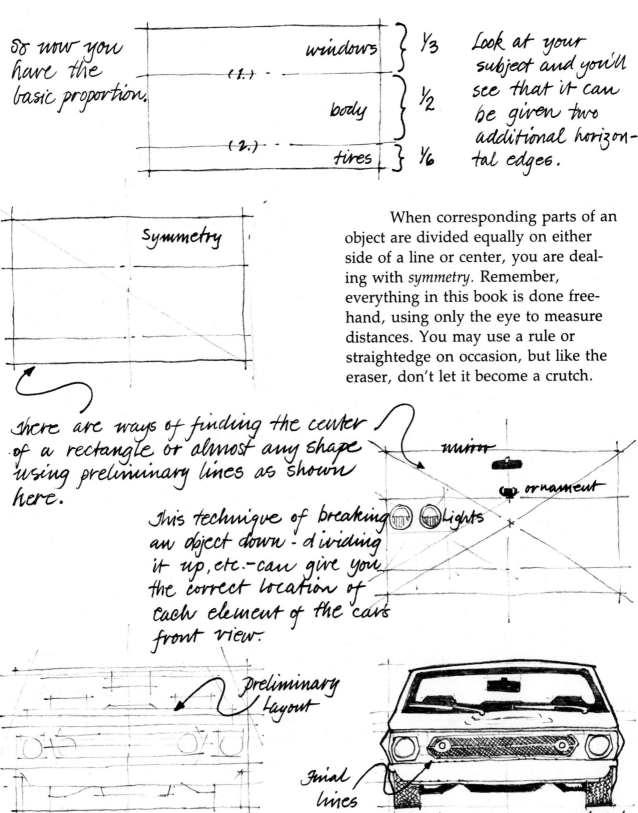

So now you have the basic proportion.

windows	}	⅓
body	}	½
tires	}	⅙

Look at your subject and you'll see that it can be given two additional horizontal edges.

Symmetry

When corresponding parts of an object are divided equally on either side of a line or center, you are dealing with *symmetry*. Remember, everything in this book is done freehand, using only the eye to measure distances. You may use a rule or straightedge on occasion, but like the eraser, don't let it become a crutch.

There are ways of finding the center of a rectangle or almost any shape using preliminary lines as shown here.

mirror

ornament

Lights

This technique of breaking an object down - dividing it up, etc.- can give you the correct location of each element of the car's front view.

Preliminary Layout

Final lines

Locating the preliminary lines is your primary concern. Sketch in these guidelines in graph-paper fashion - always concentrating on proportion. Make the preliminary lines light.

If you are planning to become a designer, artist, or illustrator, you will very probably need to know something about drawing a car. Cars, trucks, buses, trains, boats, and planes surround and fill our environment. It is not fair for professionals to represent a setting and purposely leave out these basic elements. Often cars are left out because the artist doesn't know how to draw them, but a more serious mistake occurs when, for example, an architect leaves them out because their omission makes the design (building, shopping center, etc.) look more appealing.

While drawing cars may not be your favorite pastime, drawing particular ones (such as the Gremlin) perhaps seems even less valuable. The thing to keep in mind is the *process:* proportions, preliminary lines for the major elements, and then secondary preliminary lines for minor elements. Do as many of these light lines as necessary before beginning to finalize the drawing.

There are convincing arguments put forth, especially by designers, that say that the support elements (cars, pets, furnishings) should be drawn

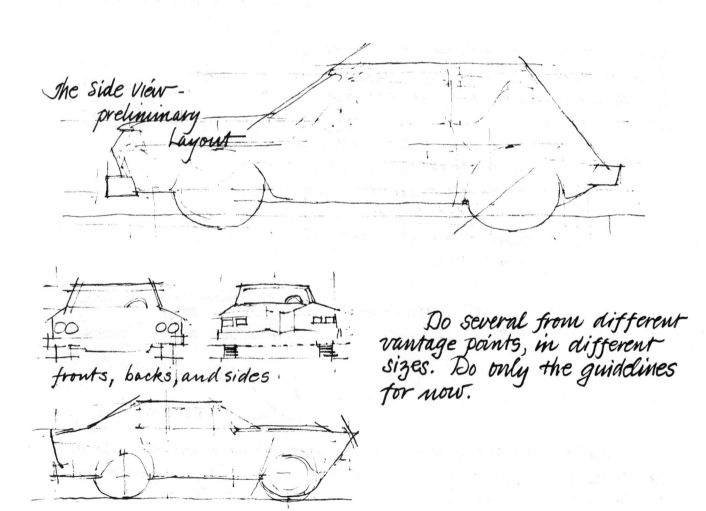

The side view - preliminary layout

fronts, backs, and sides

Do several from different vantage points, in different sizes. Do only the guidelines for now.

very simply, that they should be drawn without detail, even abstracted, unless, of course, one of these is the focus of attention. Some designers even draw their own vehicles, animals, etc., from their imagination. This is good. The danger arises when the made-up object is far wide of the mark. You can, and eventually will, use your imagination rather liberally. You will make up things. The question is, do you know enough, have you practiced enough to make them believable? It is a great risk to abstract things of which you know little and to get carried away with your inventiveness.

I'm sure you've seen many unconvincing representations. Here is my point: abstract things, simplify them, even originate unseen objects, *but* do it from a position of confidence. Know the thing. Therein lies a great secret of "style." Know the thing inside and out. Be *able* to draw all its details, and the resulting simplification will capture the essentials that cannot be compromised.

Like it is for almost everyone starting something new, you may be having some difficulties. If you are taking drawing seriously and are still

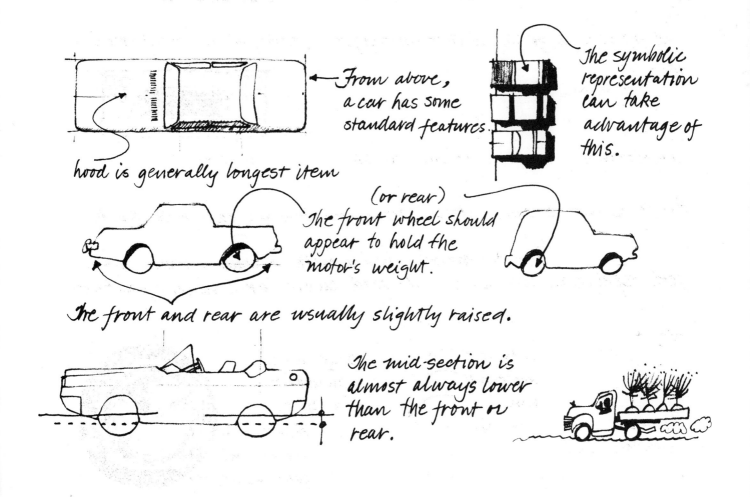

From above, a car has some standard features.

The symbolic representation can take advantage of this.

hood is generally longest item

(or rear)

The front wheel should appear to hold the motor's weight.

The front and rear are usually slightly raised.

The mid-section is almost always lower than the front or rear.

having some problems, try these pointers: first, do some warm-ups, with an emphasis on lines; second, do a few pages of just lines, turning the pages into sheets of graph paper; third, breeze back through the book and practice simple proportions of things; and fourth, break the car down into its parts and study them separately.

The door of a car could be thought of first as a simple rectangle (vertical orientation).

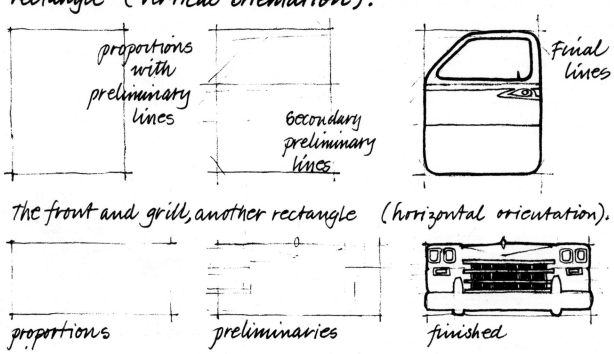

proportions with preliminary lines

Secondary preliminary lines

Final lines

The front and grill, another rectangle (horizontal orientation).

proportions   preliminaries   finished

Since a car is symmetrical, preliminaries are easier to check.

For the wheel, begin with a square unless you feel especially confident. A good circle takes much practice.

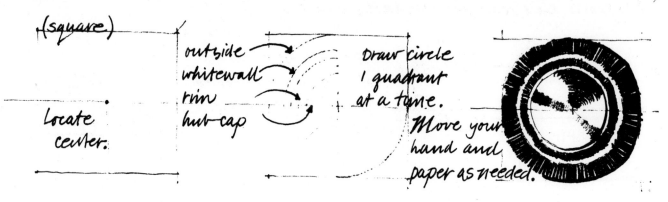

(square)

Locate center.

outside
whitewall
rim
hub cap

Draw circle 1 quadrant at a time. Move your hand and paper as needed.

The "ordinary" car is not always so ordinary, but having a good approach can help you to master difficult shapes.

Preliminary lines help you locate each major element before finalizing the drawing. However, they are not sacred. If they are not where you need them, abandon them. That is their basic purpose: to give you something on which to base your judgments.

You will notice that the drawings of the cars shown here follow the hints given earlier plus a new one I would like to now mention. It is called *line weight*, which involves varying the weight of the line to express different parts. Take a look at the various weights and notice how they contrib-

ute to the drawing. This is an old technique that artists have long employed. The heavier lines are on the edge, and they get progressively lighter (smaller) as their importance diminishes.

The *side view*, or elevation as it is often called, is likely to occupy you for a few days. Don't be concerned.

Begin now to practice outside the context of the warm-up exercises. Start drawing side views of cars. Draw the front, the rear, even the top. Start collecting photos or drawings by others; begin a scrapbook of examples. No designer/artist worth his or her salt would be caught dead without boxes of collected examples. From these you can copy or trace until your confidence improves. You are not after absolute accuracy, only a respectable representation.

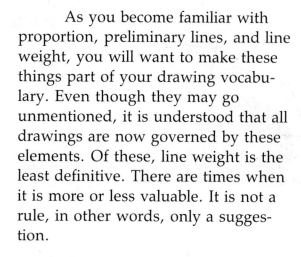

As you become familiar with proportion, preliminary lines, and line weight, you will want to make these things part of your drawing vocabulary. Even though they may go unmentioned, it is understood that all drawings are now governed by these elements. Of these, line weight is the least definitive. There are times when it is more or less valuable. It is not a rule, in other words, only a suggestion.

Here is a suggestion for applying the line weight. Have several sharpened pencils at hand. After your preliminaries are satisfactory, pick a pencil point that is medium fine (slightly rounded) and line out the car, finalizing all the important edges and all secondary elements. Leave the finer details for later. Now take a well-rounded point and go over that outermost edge. Next rub down a fine point and finish the details.

An example: In step 1 you want to draw the proportions of your subject. Sketch these in with primary preliminary lines, boxing in the subject and getting it onto the paper. In step 2, the subject is located accurately, and secondary preliminary lines begin to outline the major parts. The preliminary drawing is now complete, but very light and sketchy. In step 3, develop the lines of the subject itself; locate the details including, in this case, the setting, and manipulate the surfaces and details.

keep pencil points the way you want them by rubbing them on a spare piece of paper.

rounded

pointed

3.

'79

4.

Berkshire Builders

Manchester, New Hamshire

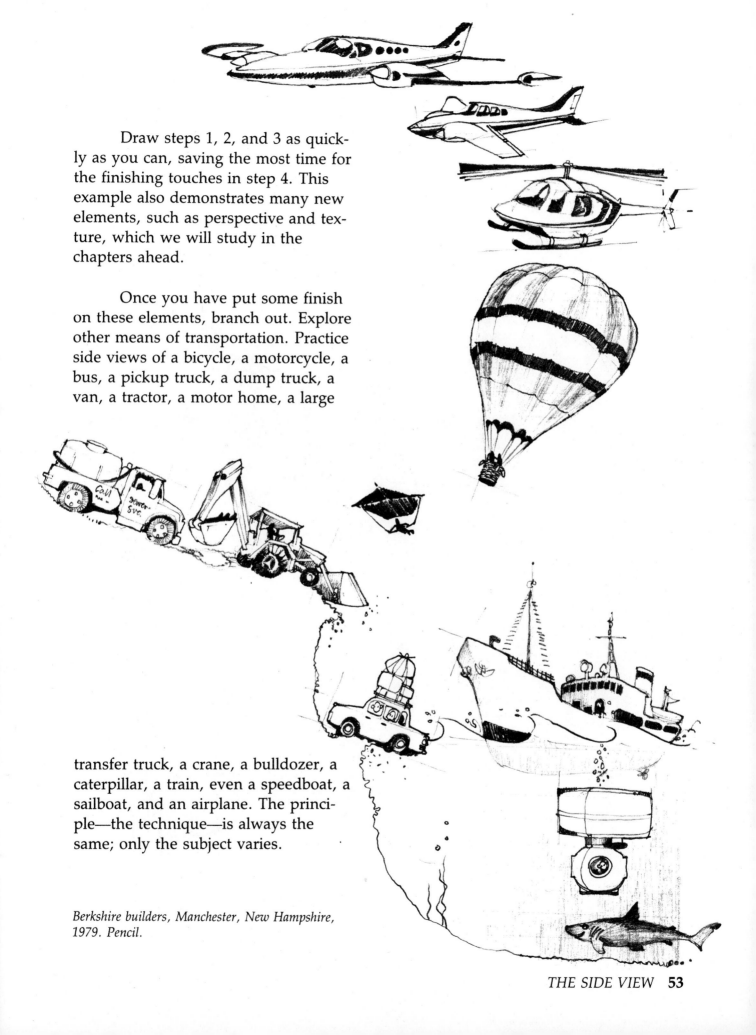

Draw steps 1, 2, and 3 as quickly as you can, saving the most time for the finishing touches in step 4. This example also demonstrates many new elements, such as perspective and texture, which we will study in the chapters ahead.

Once you have put some finish on these elements, branch out. Explore other means of transportation. Practice side views of a bicycle, a motorcycle, a bus, a pickup truck, a dump truck, a van, a tractor, a motor home, a large

transfer truck, a crane, a bulldozer, a caterpillar, a train, even a speedboat, a sailboat, and an airplane. The principle—the technique—is always the same; only the subject varies.

Berkshire builders, Manchester, New Hampshire, 1979. Pencil.

Shelley's grave, Rome, 1975. Drafting pen.

54 *DRAWING WITH CONFIDENCE*

5. Appearance and Reality

Drawing objects as they appear in reality, that is, with proper *perspective*, is the first major challenge in learning to draw. Perspective drawing, as we know it, was first employed by artists and draftsmen around the turn of the fourteenth century. That was the first time that perspective drawing was widely taught and employed by "educated" artists. Obviously, for quite a long time people wondered how to represent three-dimensional reality on a two-dimensional surface. There were some very strange things going on out there. Buildings, for example, which the artist knew quite well were just as big on one end as the other, appeared considerably smaller on the end farther from the eye.

In the Renaissance, artists began to look very intently at objects and to imagine themselves making copies of images that would approximate reality. Many elaborate schemes were put forward. One method that gained much prestige was to use a pane of glass to intercept the view being drawn. Using paper as the pane of glass, the artist drew the object just as the artist perceived it. After the principle was understood, the pane of glass could be dispensed with.

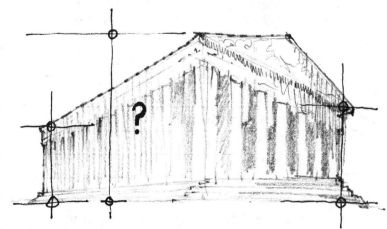

How could this be? what is going on?

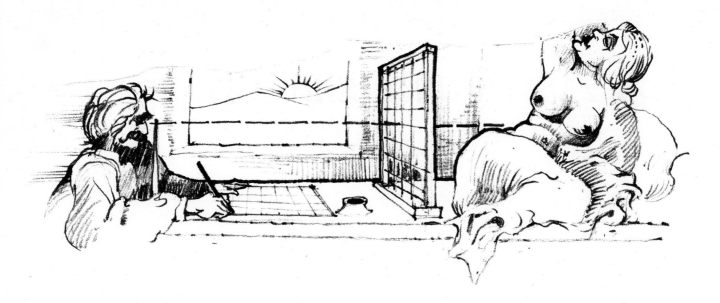

As drawing and painting commissions started pouring into these early professionals, they looked for a system whereby young apprentices could help the masters keep up with the demand for artwork. The problem was this: if an apprentice was asked to draw a cottage, he would likely do a very elementary front view. Naturally, that would never do when something not quite so flat-looking was needed.

Gyorgy Kepes discusses this phenomenon in his book *Education of Vision*. It is an interesting area of concern, especially to those educators who are teaching perspective. In a sense, each artist must relive the history of the development of perspective. Each generation of designers must go back to the Middle Ages and begin to ask basic questions. How do I make things look smaller on one end when I know they are the same size? If you are to learn to draw, you will grapple with the concept of perspective drawing, just as the ancients did.

Try this experiment yourself. Ask a child to draw a table with four places set.

you are likely to come up with something resembling this,

when in reality you know very well that the eye view looked more like this.

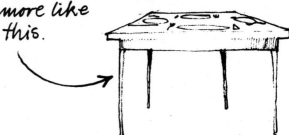

Perspective drawing is applying a man-made system to represent the things we see so that we can abstract their reality and thereby communicate their existence in the symbolic language of drawing. Now here is how the system works. It is based on a number of given qualities or ideas. The first is that of a *horizon:* for perspective purposes, it is simpler to hold with the theory that the earth is flat, the curve of the earth is imperceptible.

The example of the railroad track brings up three more points. First, all parallel lines will vanish to the same point (the steel rails). Second, if your eye is perpendicular to any set of parallel lines (the wooden ties), these will not appear to vanish to either the right or the left. Instead, as with the ties shown at the top, the spaces between them and the ends will appear to get smaller and vanish. And third, if the lines are on a flat plane (ground), they will appear to vanish to a single point on the horizon called a *vanishing point* (V. P.).

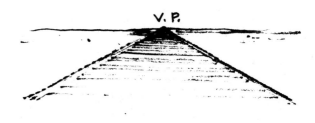

The second is that all objects appear to become smaller away from us and finally vanish, or come toward us and get larger. The classic example of this phenomenon is how a railroad track appears as you stand in the middle and look down the tracks.

Be aware that if the ground were not flat or reasonably flat the vanishing point of the parallel lines would not go to the horizon, but would instead go a comparable distance and then vanish — into the sky or below the ground.

• V.P.

V.P.

V.P.

But let's keep it simple for now and go back to the railroad tracks.

Imagine that you have stepped over to the side of the tracks and sat down on one rail.

Notice now how the rails vanish the same as before, but the ties now are taking on a vanishing aspect.

The system has another peculiar rule. Technically, once you've decided on a perspective view you wish to draw, the system assumes that your eyes don't move. If you were to move, the vanishing point and horizon would move correspondingly.

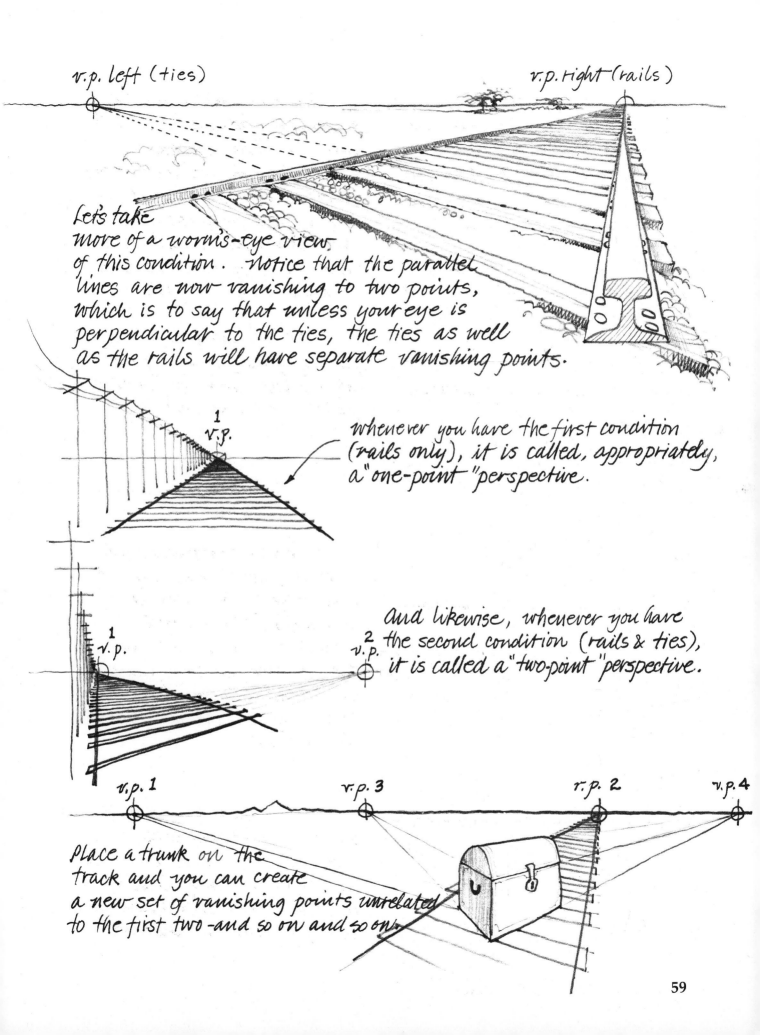

v.p. left (ties)   v.p. right (rails)

Let's take
more of a worm's-eye view
of this condition. Notice that the parallel
lines are now vanishing to two points,
which is to say that unless your eye is
perpendicular to the ties, the ties as well
as the rails will have separate vanishing points.

1
v.p.

whenever you have the first condition
(rails only), it is called, appropriately,
a "one-point" perspective.

1
v.p.

2
v.p.

And likewise, whenever you have
the second condition (rails & ties),
it is called a "two-point" perspective.

v.p. 1   v.p. 3   v.p. 2   v.p. 4

Place a trunk on the
track and you can create
a new set of vanishing points unrelated
to the first two - and so on and so on.

59

But, as I said, let's keep to the basics. "Two-point" perspective is most often used, and so we will stay close to that system.

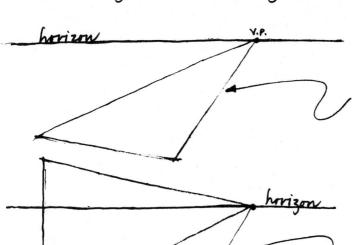

Reviewing what you have so far become familiar with, let's imagine that instead of a railroad track we have huge sheets of glass. First, if you had a sheet of glass lying on the ground, with parallel sides that went off into the distance, it would look like this.

Now let's imagine another pane of glass replacing the utility poles from the previous page. It would look like this.

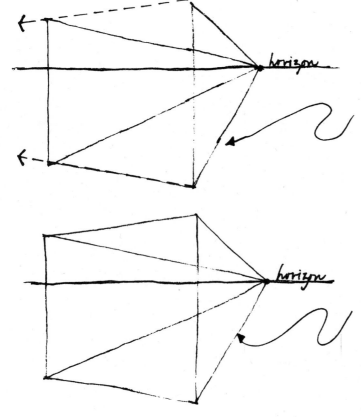

To that arrangement add another pane of glass on the right edge of the pane that is lying on the ground. It would then look like this. Notice that we still have a left vanishing point, but it is hidden off the left side of the paper.

Then finally a pane of glass on the top completes the arrangement. Can you clearly see the resulting glass tunnel? Do you understand how each side fits into the picture?

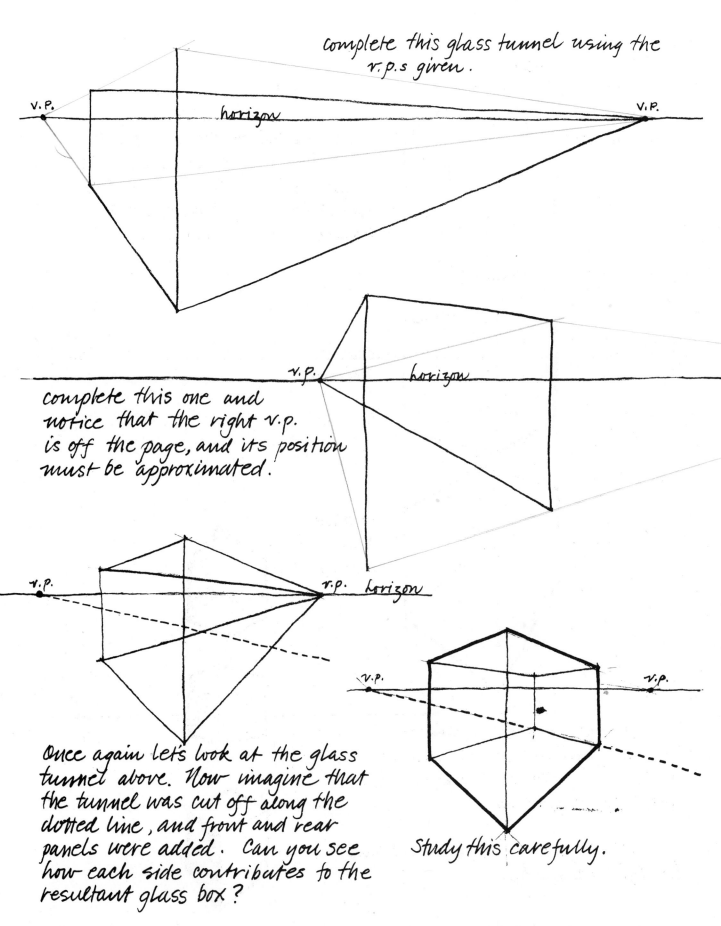

complete this glass tunnel using the
r.p.s given.

v.P.   horizon   V.P.

complete this one and
notice that the right v.p.
is off the page, and its position
must be approximated.

v.p.   horizon

v.p.   v.p. horizon

v.p.   v.p.

Once again let's look at the glass
tunnel above. Now imagine that
the tunnel was cut off along the
dotted line, and front and rear
panels were added. Can you see
how each side contributes to the
resultant glass box?

Study this carefully.

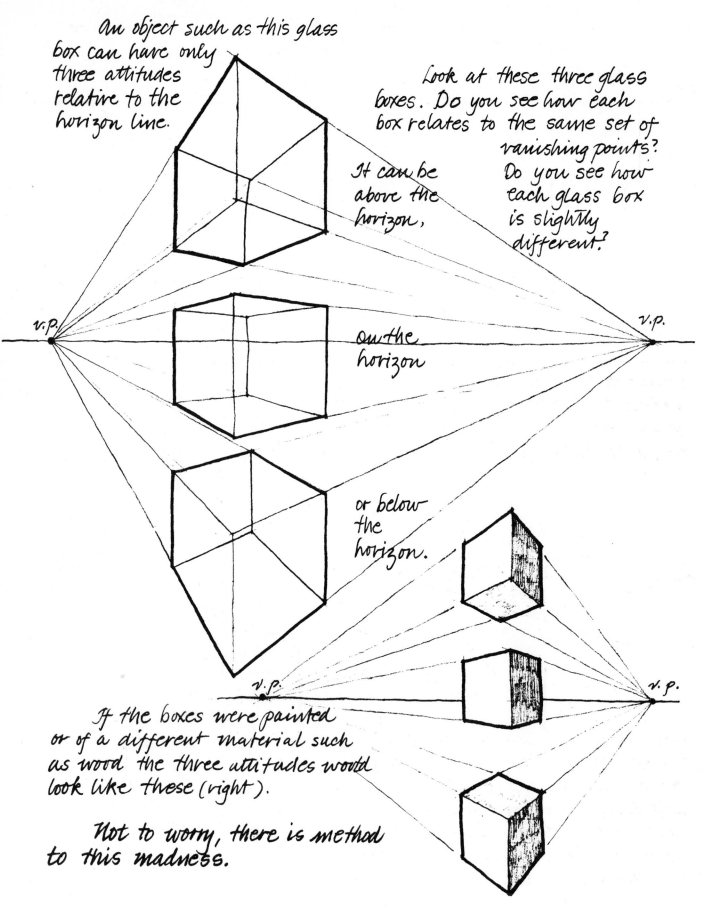

An object such as this glass box can have only three attitudes relative to the horizon line.

Look at these three glass boxes. Do you see how each box relates to the same set of vanishing points? Do you see how each glass box is slightly different?

It can be above the horizon,

v.p.

on the horizon

v.p.

or below the horizon.

v.p.

If the boxes were painted or of a different material such as wood the three attitudes would look like these (right).

Not to worry, there is method to this madness.

v.p.

Here is a good exercise. Using what you now know about perspective, fill in all the missing sides of the boxes below. When you're completed this exercise, begin doodling in perspective. Do warm-up exercises in perspective glass boxes, or make up elaborate perspective conglomerates.

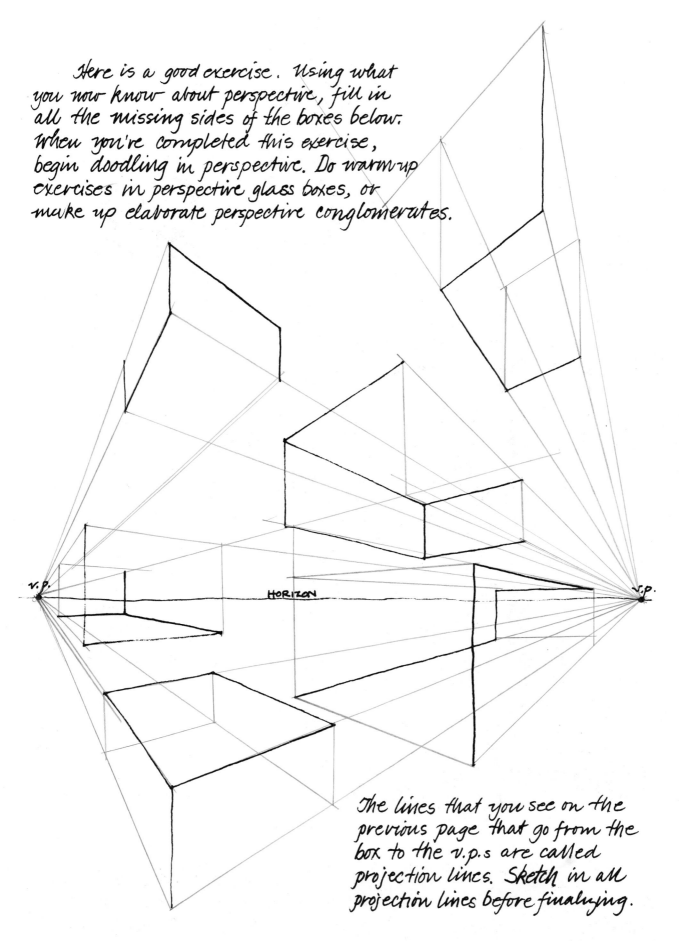

v.p.

HORIZON

v.p.

The lines that you see on the previous page that go from the box to the v.p.s are called projection lines. Sketch in all projection lines before finalizing.

Palermo, Sicily, 1976. Ball-point pen.

Notice in the sketch of a Palermo street scene how the cars are parked on an inclined plane. You must be prepared for this aspect of perspective or you will become frustrated by perspective drawing systems.

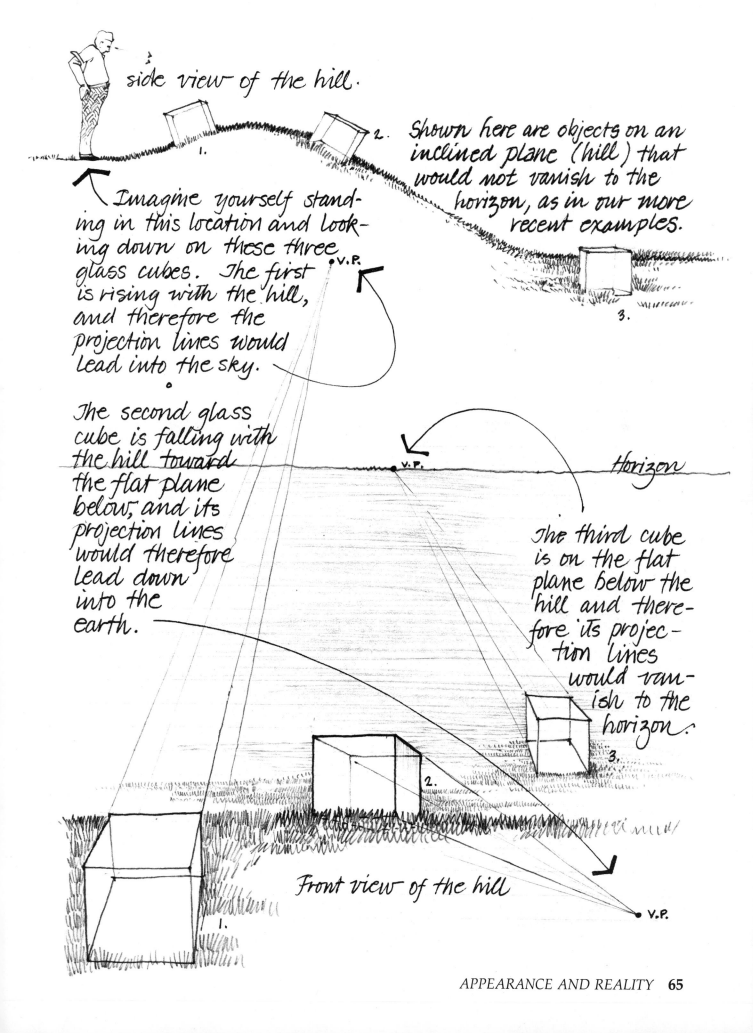

side view of the hill.

Shown here are objects on an inclined plane (hill) that would not vanish to the horizon, as in our more recent examples.

Imagine yourself standing in this location and looking down on these three glass cubes. The first is rising with the hill, and therefore the projection lines would lead into the sky.

• V.P.

The second glass cube is falling with the hill toward the flat plane below, and its projection lines would therefore lead down into the earth.

Horizon

V.P.

The third cube is on the flat plane below the hill and therefore its projection lines would vanish to the horizon.

3.

2.

Front view of the hill

• V.P.

1.

6. Horizon and the Eye

There is a fundamental relationship between the horizon and the eye. We will take a close look at that relationship in this chapter.

The first element in the perspective system you have been learning about is the *horizon*. As long as you are earthbound (say within seven miles of the surface), the horizon will play an important part in the perspective-drawing system.

horizon

horizon

Dragon Valley, Ravello, 1976. Felt pen.

Many perspective-drawing apprentices, after hearing so much about the horizon, are a bit anxious when they sit down to draw and see no horizon before them.

In the sketches of the house and the office shown here, the horizon cannot be seen. It must be imagined and scored in very lightly. If you were to remove all the obstacles in front of the view—the house, the office, the trees, and any intervening landscape—the horizon would be back there in plain view. Since this is not practical,

If you lived near the sea or on an open prairie, the horizon would be quite clear.

horizon

we must often satisfy ourselves with an imaginary line representing the horizon.

The horizon can be in two other more unusual positions. Don't let this throw you — the principle is the same. First, it can be above your view.

_ _ _ _ _ _ _ _ _ _ horizon _ _ _ _ _ r.P.⊕

This is how an artist can project himself into the air. Place the horizon above the paper; a bird's-eye view results.

The vanishing points must naturally be off of the paper.

The second position, as you might have guessed, is below your view. In this case you are looking up, and you have chosen a view that must place the horizon below your paper.

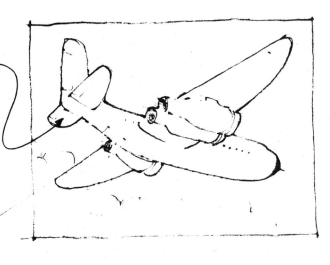

_ _ ⊕r.P. _horizon_ _ _ _ _ _ _ _ _ _ _ _ _ _ _ _ _ _

Typically, an artist will place a light line representing the horizon on his paper or wherever so that he can locate the v.p.s and the system can prevail. More often than not, in actual practice you will not be able to see the horizon directly.

Atmospheric conditions, fog, rain, low-light levels, smog, etc. will pose additional obstacles to locating the horizon.

There is an easy way to know exactly where the horizon is. It follows your eye level. In other words, whatever level your eyes are, in relation to an object, the horizon always is at that same level.

Lets' say you are standing looking at a large board. The horizon intersects the board coincidental with your eye level (5').

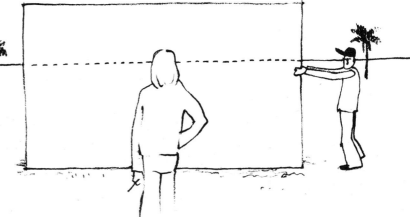

you pull in a ladder and climb up to peer over the board. There is the horizon.

so you lie down to view the board from only inches off the ground, and there too you find the horizon faithfully waiting.

Thus, if you could not see the horizon in relation to an object that you wanted to draw, you would know exactly where to place the line representing the horizon - at the level of your eyes. Ask yourself this question: "How far are my eyes from the ground in relation to the object?" The answer tells you where to draw the line.

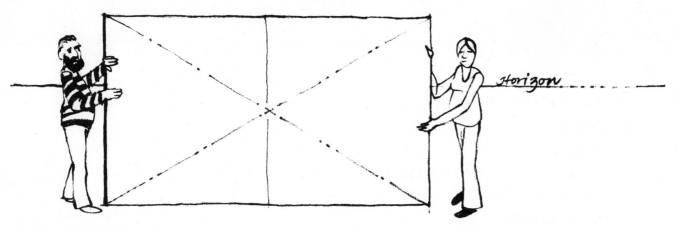

Looking back for a moment at the large board, notice what happens when we devide it in half and then swing one end away from your view.

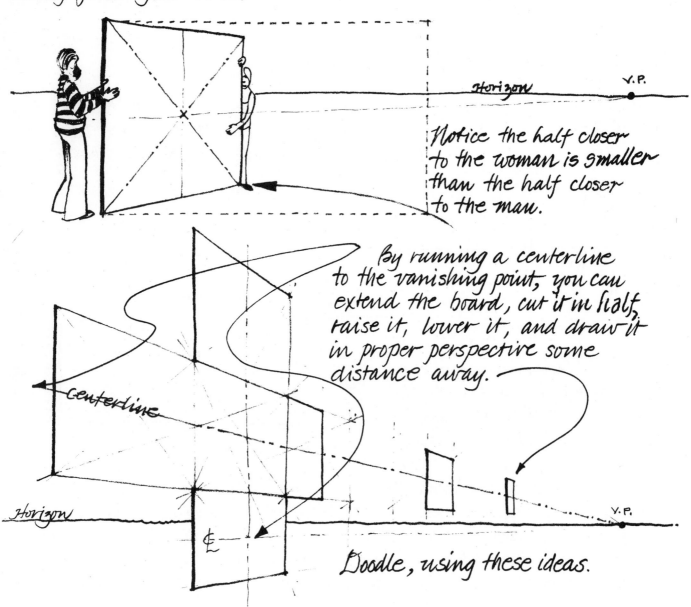

Notice the half closer to the woman is smaller than the half closer to the man.

By running a centerline to the vanishing point, you can extend the board, cut it in half, raise it, lower it, and draw it in proper perspective some distance away.

Doodle, using these ideas.

S. Domenico, Siena, 1975. Brown felt pen.
(Courtesy of Viola Swedel)

Now you have a good number of the basics of freehand perspective. Two-point perspective is the foundation of freehand drawing.

Review these points and practice their application. All objects except those perpendicular to the eye will appear to vanish. Those objects on a relatively flat plane will vanish to a point on the horizon. These points can be anywhere in the field of vision and out of it (off the paper). All parallel objects, surfaces, lines, etc., have the same vanishing point. Parallel objects above or below the horizon can vanish to the horizon line. Vanishing points can be above or below the horizon, depending upon the inclination of the surface where an object sits. The horizon is always at eye level. The horizon can be seen, or it may be hidden. The horizon can be above, below, or on your drawing paper. Vanishing points can be off your paper in any direction.

Let's return for a while to those cars and see if we can find some practical application for the things you now know about perspective.

To draw this old VW bus you will want to get comfortable in your chair - take out your supplies - warm-up - Now on a clean piece of paper about ⅓ up from the bottom you draw a long light line. This is the horizon. Your eye level is just above the nearest headlight, or roughly 24" high. Draw a vertical line that represents this nearest corner. Remember proportions. Okay, proportion the 24" below the horizon line to the amount above the horizon line. Measure by eyeballing it. Cut the line off at these two points: A & B. This line roughly estimates the total height of the bus in relation to the horizon line. So this is what you have so far.

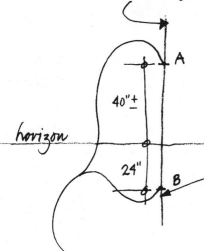

preliminary line for the nearest corner of bus

A

40"±

horizon

24"

B

A

horizon

24"

B

The eye level is the distance from the ground to your eye.

you

24" eyelevel

bus

Here is how the two lines you have relate to the scene you're about to draw.

horizon

The next thing to do is to find the two vanishing points. Pretending that you are sitting at the crossroads of two railroad tracks, point parallel to each side of the bus.

Here is how that might look if you were actually at the crossroads of two railroad tracks. By pointing or pretending to point, your arms create a steel rail parallel to the front and side of the bus. This is a visual guess, but if you've been practicing proportions you can get close enough.

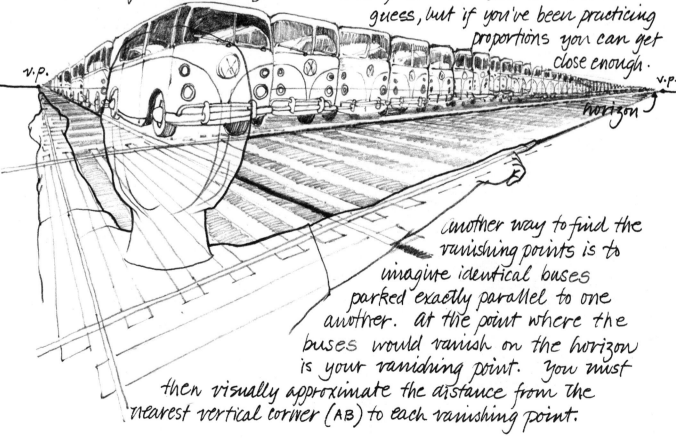

v.p.

v.p.

horizon

Another way to find the vanishing points is to imagine identical buses parked exactly parallel to one another. At the point where the buses would vanish on the horizon is your vanishing point. You must then visually approximate the distance from the nearest vertical corner (AB) to each vanishing point.

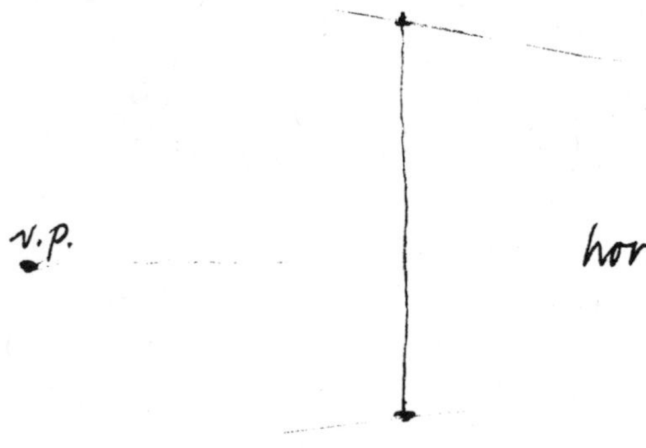

at this point we have four things:
the horizon line, the nearest corner
of the bus, the left v.p., and the right v.p.

v.p.

horizon

v.p.

now, lightly project lines from the top and
bottom of the nearest corner to the two v.p.s.

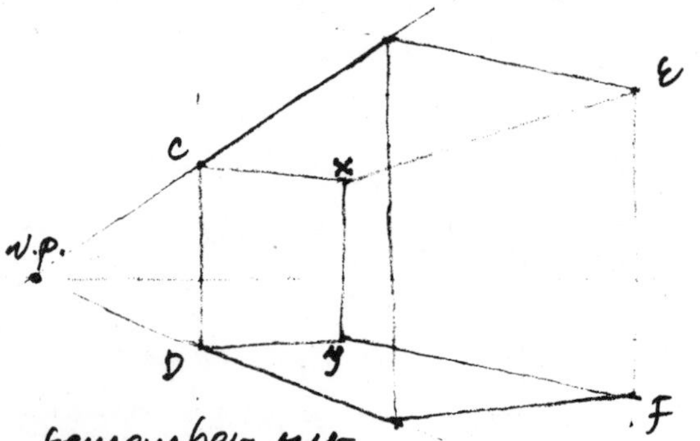

c

E

x

v.p.

horizon

v.p.

D

y

.F

remember our
glass boxes?

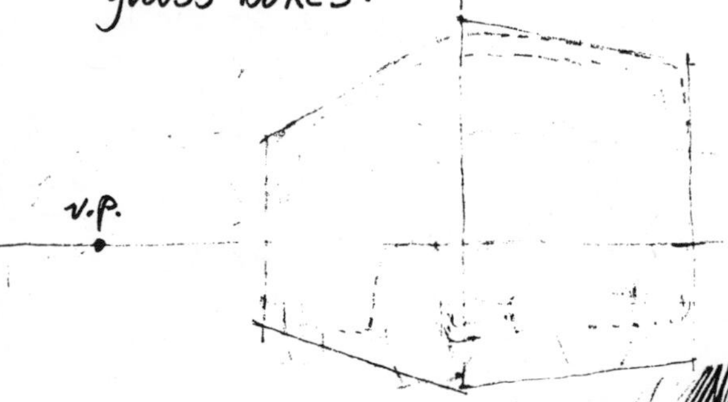

Along the two sets of projection
lines, look at the bus and
visually score lines CD & EF.

These lines represent the outer
edges of the bus. Project them
back and form the invisible far
corner of the bus, x & y.

v.p.

horizon

v.p.

Lightly sketch in, in much
the same fashion as in chapter
4 (The Side View), all necessary
preliminary lines.

Add finishing touches and there
you have it. A drawing in
two-point perspective.

Let's review those steps briefly, and remember that each time you follow through on a perspective sequence you will find shortcuts. You will find ways to avoid steps that you may now be struggling with. Assuming you are not quite that advanced yet, here are the steps to remember:

1. Get comfortable and pick your view.

2. Draw the horizon lightly.

3. Draw a vertical line that represents the nearest corner.

4. Proportion the amount of the object that is below and above the horizon line.

5. Mark these points on the vertical line.

6. Find the vanishing points.

7. Mark these points lightly on the horizon line in proportion to the vertical line.

8. Project light lines from the top and bottom of the vertical line to each vanishing point.

9. Along these projection lines visually determine the width and depth of the object.

10. Score these points with new vertical lines, cutting off the object in its proper place.

11. Repeat these steps as necessary for other objects or aspects of the original object.

12. Using the vanishing points as needed, lightly sketch in all preliminary details.

13. Add finishing lines.

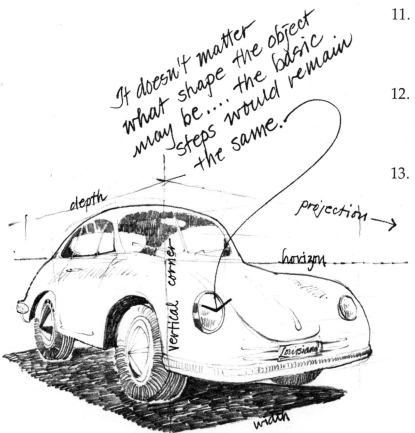

It doesn't matter what shape the object may be.... the basic steps would remain the same.

depth

projection →

horizon

vertical corner

width

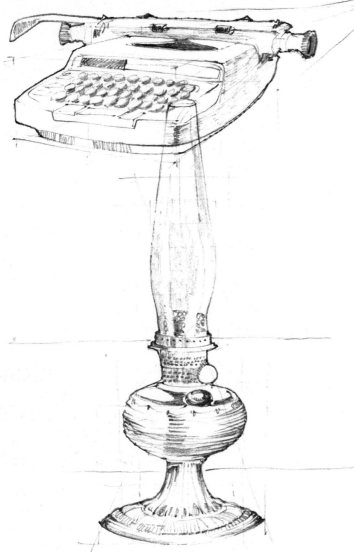

Besides drawing lots of perspective doodles, in between more serious sessions such as the exercise we just completed, draw the ordinary things around you. Draw a collection of things that you have on your desk or in your room. Employ the perspective system, using only the basic elements. First draw a light line representing the horizon. This is at eye level (your eyes). How does your eye level relate to the object you're about to draw? Now rough in a box that vanishes appropriately. Think of the object you are going to draw as if it were in a cardboard box. After this layout, begin the primary and secondary preliminary lines. Get things the way you want them lightly first. Now add the final touches.

Perspective is not easy, so practice is essential. As you are gaining control over perspective, don't forget earlier work with proportion and line weight.

Practice perspective using the ordinary things around you.

Joyce Hensley. On the Road. *Pencil. (Courtesy of the artist)*

7. Overlapping

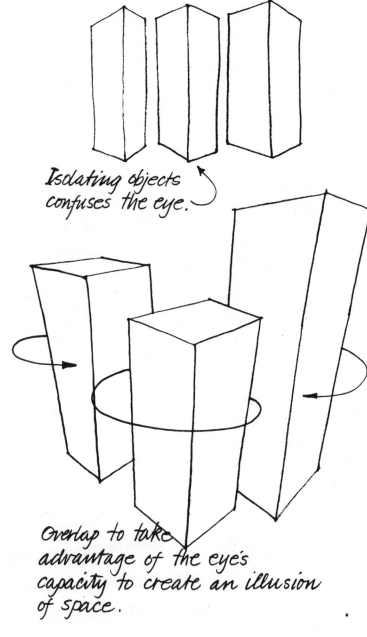

Isolating objects confuses the eye.

Overlap to take advantage of the eye's capacity to create an illusion of space.

Before going on to another study area, I would like to introduce a trick that has historically trespassed on almost every art style. It is a rather modest but important trick that relates to our conception of three-dimensional space. It is called *overlapping*. Because we know that space (air, atmosphere) surrounds all objects, overlapping can aid in the sense of three-dimensional reality. What you know about the real world you will transfer to a drawing situation. This helps to explain why some art is disturbing—it breaks the rules of what we think we know about reality. Many artists distort or arrange drawings to consciously manipulate reality: chairs pitched unnaturally, people and objects isolated from one another, and so on. But the fact is that objects are seldom isolated; they usually are a part of a mass of other objects. Most things are themselves partly hidden, or they are in turn overlapping something else. Many students have a tendency to isolate objects and draw them as victims before a firing squad. Overlap things whenever or wherever possible. This is almost always an appropriate device.

start with cars, truck, bikes, etc. Draw several sets overlapping one another.

Connaught Circle, New Delhi, 1976. Brown felt pen.

8. Trees and Other Plants

Proceeding with the objective—
drawing with confidence—you must
now add trees and other plants to
your repertoire.

Piazza A. Monzoni, Siena, 1975. Ball-point pen.

Thomas Gainsborough. Landscape. *Charcoal, estompe, heightened with white chalk, on blue paper. (Courtesy of The Metropolitan Museum of Art, Rogers Fund, 1907)*

Trees in particular are the single most dominant aspect of the living landscape. The relationship between trees and art is a very ancient one. People have long revered trees and have used them as symbols of life, representing stability, endurance, and permanence. That is why a simple drawing of a tree can be so stirring. It speaks to us of our oldest, even unconscious, yearning—to be one with nature.

In drawing trees and other plants, you can benefit directly from an intensive session with the exercises discussed earlier. Why? Because, among other things, plant drawings are dependent upon *texture*. Texture is the "feel" of a surface: rough, smooth, fine, slippery, granular, coarse, etc. And texture is the result of the parts of an object contributing to the overall effect. In a tree, for example, the individual leaves gather to display a coarse, medium, or fine textured mass.

 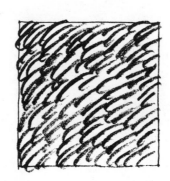 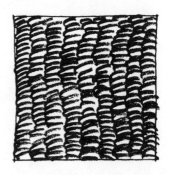

About the most useful textural stroke is the "c" curve (above). Practice this stroke regularly. I must warn you that almost nothing will tire you so quickly as having to sit and draw the individual leaves of a tree. So you must first build your confidence by mastering some of the fundamental textures.

Notice that the emphasis on line drawing is giving way to the more subtle techniques of shading - creating textures.

An excellent way to start drawing trees and other plants is to first practice drawing their textures.

Your goal in practically all drawing is what I call *symbolic representation*. What you want to accomplish is a believable substitute for reality. I would like, for one moment, to underline the value of realistic drawing—a serious reminder. If you haven't already, think a minute about what you are doing. You are abstracting three-dimensional reality onto a two-dimensional surface. You are doing it with very sophisticated symbols, and what is more, you have grown so comfortable with it that it holds little awe. You are to be congratulated. Drawing anything is a complex maneuver. It is an abstraction. And drawing "realistically" is in itself one of man's most abstract activities.

  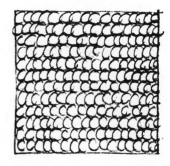

Here are several texture exercises that I have found especially useful: the umbrella, the saucer, and the continuous "c" curve. Notice that the pencil is moving rapidly without pause.

 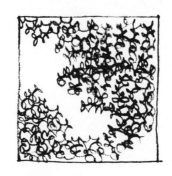 

Another texture to practice is the "squiggle." Squiggles should range from random to uniform and from nervous to highly controlled. Invent squiggles based on careful observation of different plants.

  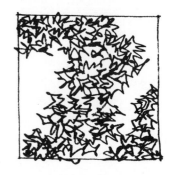

One of your main objectives in these texture exercises is to increase speed. Set up challenges for yourself. Draw the squares within which you are going to practice textures, decide on what stroke you want to practice, then fill the squares working for speed and control. Speed is an artist's salvation from tedious chores.

Dewitt County, Illinois. Pencil. (Courtesy of Johnson, Johnson & Roy, Landscape Architects)

In drawing plants you will find that some strokes are particularly suited to certain plants, such as grasses, pines, and junipers.

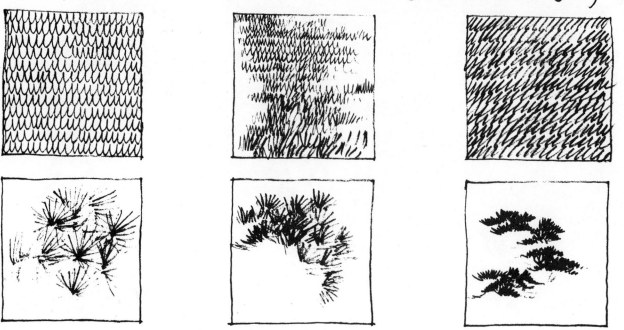

Because plants are such fundamental aspects of our lives, drawing them is an essential element of any comprehensive art training. Plants define our spaces, provide us shade, act as protectors from wind, noise, and dust. They reduce glare and summer's heat and give us seasonal interest through blossoms, growth, and fall colors. They serve our eyes as things to see in themselves or as a backdrop for the viewing of other elements. There is no need to list all their virtues, because, aside from their practicality, plants are simply beautiful and a great joy to behold. Consider Wu Chen's brush. This is perhaps *the* reason to draw at all.

Umbrella pines, Rome, 1975. Felt pen.

Wu Chen. Bamboo in the Wind. *Sung Dynasty, 960–1279. (Courtesy of the Museum of Fine Arts, Boston)*

A likely beginning for plants would be their details. Study them closely and draw small areas, paying attention first to detail.

a large tree meeting the ground, grasses, and small plants

The natural ground debris

Leaf textures

Alternate drawing details close and then far away. Several days would be well spent studying details.

branching

Tool shed, 1975. Brown felt pen. (Courtesy of Helen Sandifer)

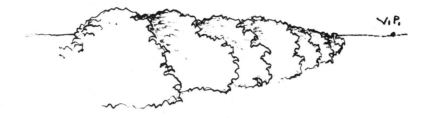

Before going further into drawing trees and other plants, I would like to introduce a few new ideas and perhaps review some of the earlier ones. *Proportion*, as it relates to plants, is much the same as we studied earlier.

Perspective, as it relates to plants, works in two ways primarily. First, consider the more mechanical aspect: things get smaller with distance from the eye toward a vanishing point.

Second, and perhaps more important, is an item called textural perspective: things get small across their surface. That is to say that the leaves at the top of a tree would be smaller than those closer to your eye at the bottom of the tree.

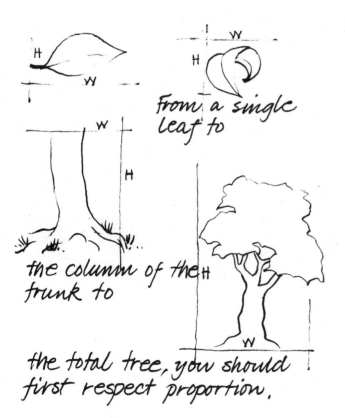

from a single leaf to

the column of the trunk to

the total tree, you should first respect proportion.

Lake edge. Pencil. (Courtesy of Johnson, Johnson & Roy, Landscape Architects)

Now that might seem a rather obvious observation, but the value here is that with your knowledge of textural perspective you can exaggerate and thereby increase a viewer's ability to accept the three-dimensional nature of your two-dimensional drawing.

Textural perspective is an especially useful tool for grasses.

9. The Sun and Other Allies

One of drawing's most dependable allies needs little introduction. *Light* is the ultimate source of our perceptions. Primarily I am referring to sunlight, but other light sources are not excluded.

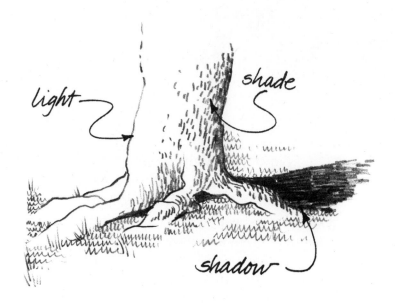

Working on the windows, 1982. Felt pen.

Because the sun is so huge and so far away, its rays are perceived as being essentially parallel to one another. This simplifies our understanding of how they work to form *shade* and *shadow*. Before your drawings can take on meaningful textures, you must become aware of the role sunlight plays in creating the textures you see.

The surface that is exposed to the sunlight will naturally reflect that light to your eyes. Objects will be lightest on the sun side. Your texture decisions must reflect an understanding of this principle. Note that *shade* exists when a surface is turned away from the light.

Shadow exists when a surface is facing the light but is prevented from receiving light by some intervening object.

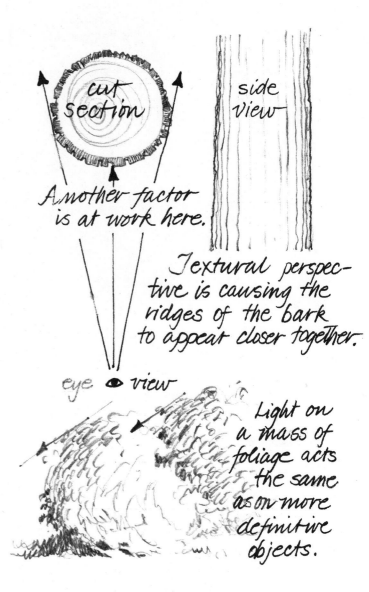

cut section

side view

Another factor is at work here.

Textural perspective is causing the ridges of the bark to appear closer together.

eye ⬤ view

Light on a mass of foliage acts the same as on more definitive objects.

Another light condition can influence the appearance of rounded or irregular-shaped objects. This is even light from the front, which causes shade to occur on both sides and at times on the top and bottom of an object.

Pencil drawings depend on the direct manipulation of black versus white: the black of the pencil and the white of the paper, the shades and shadows against the areas of light.

Notice that in the above branching arrangement contrast is used arbitrarily to help your eye separate the elements.

This idea of contrast is not limited to small details, and you should begin to employ it in a variety of different ways.

This manipulation of light and dark is often referred to as *contrast*. The use of contrast in pencil drawings very often respects the source of light, but here we have somewhat of an exception. Since you have only black versus white (and shades), contrast can also become a trick. All artists/illustrators are guilty of simply arranging contrast to their advantage. Again, one major goal is communication. Use whatever means are available if you want others to "see."

Shore pine, 1973. Charcoal. (Courtesy of H. Alva Brumfield)

An idea that we will return to in later chapters and that I would like to now offer is the matter of *line quality.* You have perhaps already noticed that the lines have taken on some character that they didn't have in previous chapters. This character is called line quality. Trees and other plants depend upon line quality to express, among other things, their natural character. A plant is a collection of growing cells always elongating, pushing, and becoming a trunk, a branch, a limb, a twig, and a bud, in that order. The stroke of a pencil has the special potential to symbolize this sequence. Practice qualitative lines.

10. Techniques for Drawing Trees

There are three techniques for drawing trees: silhouette, structure, and shading. In most drawings these ideas are usually mixed together in varying proportions, but for now let's look at them one at a time.

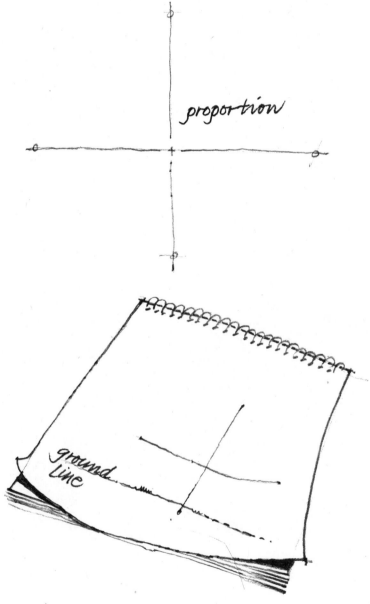

Silhouette is a method by which you concentrate on the plant's outline. Let's imagine that we have before us a normal old tree, sort of squatty and a veteran of some respectable variety of life experiences. First, you represent the proportions. Make some approximation of its height in relation to its width. If you are going to deal with the whole thing, draw in two light lines. Get your mind into the act and imagine the tree already drawn on your paper. Where is it going to be? These two lines show how large your drawing will be. They can locate as well the mass of the tree—imaginary lines of balance. Where is its vertical center? Where is its horizontal center? Add a ground line for good measure.

To these two lines add the mass of the tree—the large clumps of leaves that make up the overall form. Refer to the drawing on the previous page to see how I arrive at these clumps. Look at trees and ask yourself, "If I had to break the foliage into only five parts and thereby represent the tree, where would my dividing lines have to be?"

Now, concentrate on the outline. Notice the edge of the tree and see how it cuts against the sky. What does this edge look like? What line would best represent it? The edge tells us what kind of tree it is, if the leaves are large or small, and if the plant is near or far.

Fill in the mass with an even light or dark stroke to achieve the silhouette. Draw as quickly as you can without sacrificing control, and keep your hand and arm relaxed. Silhouette is a useful tool in a variety of circumstances, and we'll go into those aspects soon.

Structure, the second technique for drawing trees, is a method by which you concentrate on what holds the plant together. A tree, and for that matter almost all plants, can be broken down into four categories: primary leader or trunk; primary branches (main branches); secondary branches; and tertiary branches (twigs and buds).

A slightly more indirect way of looking at a tree is to compare it to your hand. I mention this simplification because many people look at trees in utter confusion, and at a glance the snarl of branches can be overwhelming. But pause and consider it calmly. It is much like a hand. The forearm first, then the hand (metacarpus) is like the main branches followed by the fingers and fingertips. Remembering this comparison, look at trees with this question in mind: Which elements must remain in order to express its simplest structure?

Many artists and teachers will tell you what to include, how to include it, and what it should look like, but few will wisely advise you on what to leave out. That is truly one of drawing's most elusive skills—simplify, simplify, simplify. But, the trick is to do it creatively in order to not lose an important detail or a telling idea.

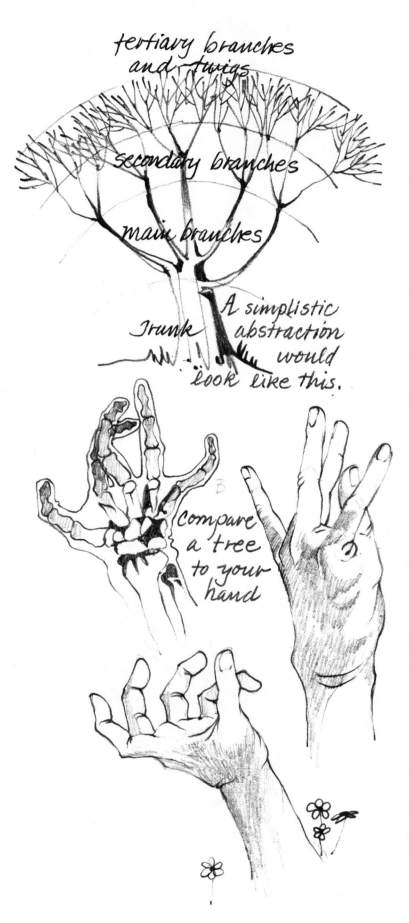

tertiary branches and twigs

secondary branches

main branches

Trunk

A simplistic abstraction would look like this.

compare a tree to your hand

Work from life and from pictures on this matter of structure. Practice drawing different types of plants. Observe them with a keen and concentrating eye. You'll find several advantages in using structure. First, it helps you to really understand and appreciate the skeleton that supports the heavy foliage. Second, you can quickly get a special effect such as cold, winter, or bareness. Third, it is quick.

We'll go over other points soon, but keep in mind that most often you are not after a duplication of a particular tree but rather a reasonable representation.

The last method, *shading*, is achieved by emphasizing light and texture.

In this field was an absolute mess of bare branches. I eliminated over 50% of them, and you can see that it is still very complex. Overlay this or draw it again to get at the basic structure more clearly.

Light acts on a tree much the same as it would on a golf ball on a tee. Notice that the darkness (*shade*) increases as the surface of the ball rotates away from the light.

This same thing happens to a tree. But because of the relative complexity of a tree, you must observe it carefully. The texture would respond to the light to indicate the size of leaves or the kind of bark or what have you. I prefer to break the surface down at first into four categories: first, full sunlight showing little or no texture; second, a slight bit of texture as the shades begin to appear; third, a moderate amount of shade as the tree

begins turning away from the light; and fourth, some good, crisp, dark pencil textures.

By expanding your repertoire with trees and other plants, you'll find that your confidence has also expanded. Drawing trees and other plants has a special way of uniting us with natural things from which we can otherwise be so widely separated.

George Inness. September Afternoon, 1887. *Oil on canvas. (Courtesy of National Collection of Fine Arts, Smithsonian Institution, Gift of William T. Evans)*

Emory Smith's hilltop, 1977. Ink. (Courtesy of Dr. Neil Odenwald)

Drawing plants will demand an investigation of texture, especially through doodling exercises and a search for the "feel" of a plant. Drawing trees requires a commitment to essentials and an acceptance of the inherent abstraction of all drawing regardless of the degree of realism.

A good place to begin drawing plants is their details, such as leaves, bark, roots, and branches. To draw plants, you must take into account contrast, light, textural perspective, shade and shadow, and line quality. Finally, there are at least three good methods to draw the whole tree: silhouette, structure, and shading. These then are the technical points. They should serve to get you started with your own work.

Notice that an artist will often combine these technical points to serve his or her own purpose. Sometimes he will mix them somewhat arbitrarily and at other times he will capture a scene that naturally contains a rich variety. These are the kinds of trails you can now pursue.

If you are interested in carrying your studies further, I would recommend Rex Vicat Cole's *The Artistic Anatomy of Trees.* It is a highly informative little book first published in 1915. There is, however, no substitute for your own drawings, done regularly with an eye for essentials and a hand made sure through confidence.

Bamiyan, Afghanistan, 1976. Ink.

11. *Landforms*

Landforms, water, clouds, and sky in freehand drawing can be quite elusive and vague. Few references exist on these subjects, although a number of good books touch on one or another of these important topics. You might say that this is a bit of new ground, so we will have to feel our way along.

Let's begin with land (ground). The ground is our first and most important stabilizing force. Being able to draw it is naturally very important. When you review the work of the landscape painters you find a great emphasis on landform. Nicolas Poussin, Corot, Inness, Thomas Cole, Homer, and Turner, among others,

developed a deep sensitivity to the land. Why were they so dedicated to it? Among other things, it gave their work such substance—such gravity. It spoke of an earlier swing back to nature—nature as a source of calm and inspiration. Artists are not alone in needing to come to terms with landforms. Architects, landscape architects, illustrators, and other designers need to include this valuable foundation element.

An understanding of and commitment to overall flatness is a significant step in mastering landforms. Landforms, even dramatic ones, are founded or seem to sit on a flat base.

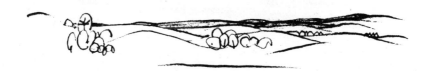

At the more detailed level, this implies "horizontalness." This horizontalness is central to the drawing tool's ability to symbolize the ground. One trick you can employ to achieve an immediate sensation of horizontalness is to sling the pencil back and forth in a more or less arbitrary fashion.

In actual practice these seemingly arbitrary strokes perform an important symbolic function. They symbolize the irregularities, the shadows, and the flatness that is the ground. Even when the textural strokes themselves are vertical, as in grass, you will want to strive for an overall effect of level, stable, and horizontal landform. Notice how this also involves textural perspective. This applies to landforms just as it would to leaves, bricks, or grass.

Rembrandt. View of London, *c. 1640. Pen and bistre, wash, white body color.*

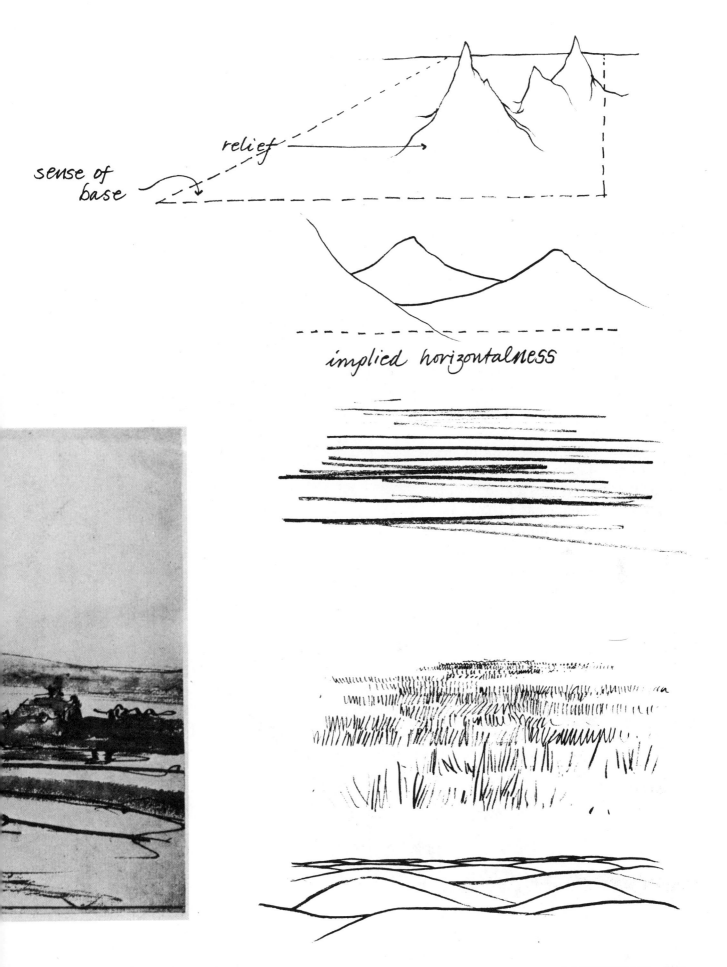

sense of base

relief

implied horizontalness

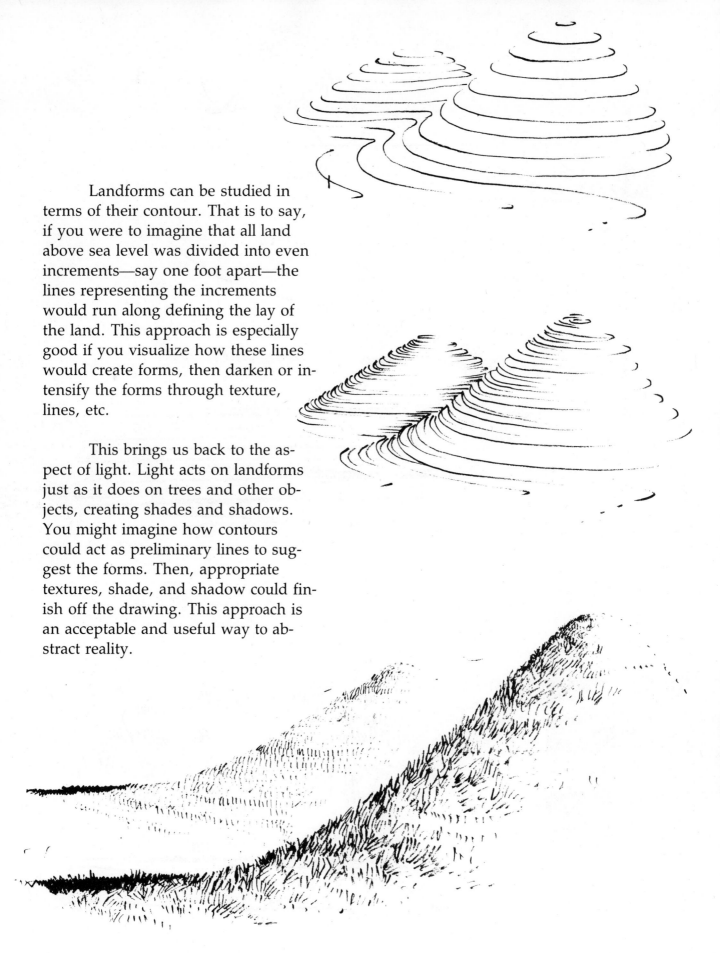

Landforms can be studied in terms of their contour. That is to say, if you were to imagine that all land above sea level was divided into even increments—say one foot apart—the lines representing the increments would run along defining the lay of the land. This approach is especially good if you visualize how these lines would create forms, then darken or intensify the forms through texture, lines, etc.

This brings us back to the aspect of light. Light acts on landforms just as it does on trees and other objects, creating shades and shadows. You might imagine how contours could act as preliminary lines to suggest the forms. Then, appropriate textures, shade, and shadow could finish off the drawing. This approach is an acceptable and useful way to abstract reality.

Villa Pamphili, Rome, 1975. Felt pen.

Information behind the object,

along the object,

and in front of the object is a good drawing aid.

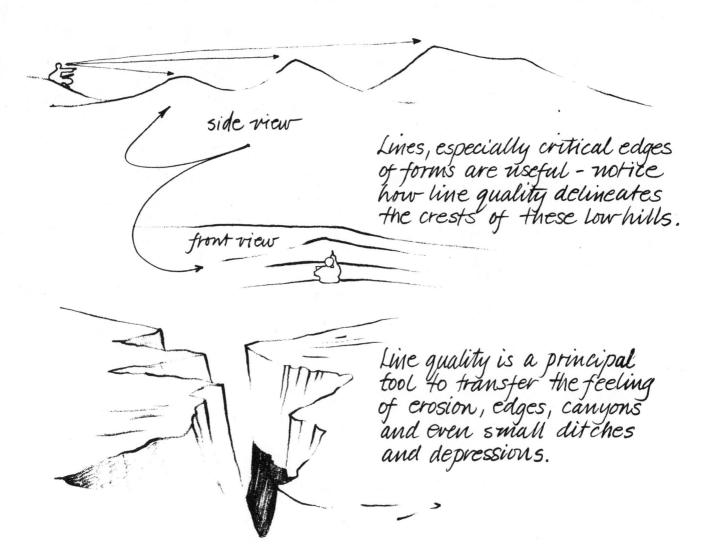

side view

front view

Lines, especially critical edges of forms are useful - notice how line quality delineates the crests of these low hills.

Line quality is a principal tool to transfer the feeling of erosion, edges, canyons and even small ditches and depressions.

There are a number of other techniques (tricks) that are helpful. For example, the shadows cast by objects onto the ground can hint at or allude to the flow and form of the land. Notice too how earlier practice is coming into play—the horizontalness of the strokes within the shadow itself. These details help to lay the land down and make it the stabilizing element it should be.

Generally you will not only want to use textural perspective, but you will want to relate it to some object or another. I have seen this trick used often. By doing this you aid once again the illusion of three-dimensional space. As a minimum, the ground should be well established in front of the object, alongside, and then behind.

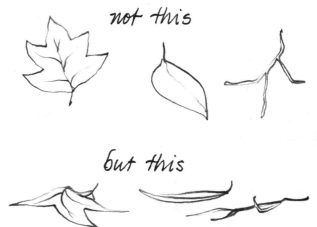

Objects lying on the ground—leaves, dead weeds, sticks, and other miscellaneous items—should be recognized as lying flat. Recognize the variety and interest. Notice that the ground is actually a dynamic partner to the other elements in a drawing. It is covered with all shapes and sizes of objects—leaves moving about with the wind, sunlight dancing over the surface, shadows of trees, buildings, clouds. It is active. Observe it carefully and then make it a positive part of your work.

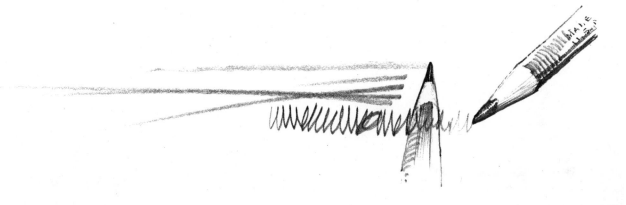

An aerial view of the landscape emphasizes the requirement that your pencil stroke be essentially flat.

Michigan, 1969. Pencil.

Theodore Kautzky. Bridge, Dinan, Brittany, *c.
1930. Broadside pencil. (Courtesy of Van Nostrand
Reinhold Company)*

12. Water

Notice that the reflection, though diagonal on the water, is done with horizontal strokes.

An effective trick is to concentrate on the edge, laying in the container very carefully and leaving the flat water to play its own role.

Except for waterfalls and fountains, drawing water has many similarities to drawing the ground. Water is another of the great calming or stabilizing aspects of landscape drawing. I have found three significant factors important in representing this aspect of the landscape. First, it is necessary to capture the flatness of water. It is absolutely horizontal. If a diagonal line must be introduced, even *it* must be achieved by fundamentally flat strokes. One early problem that many artists run into is artificially placing their eyes too high over the water they are about to draw. If you are going to draw a stream or pond, look at the vertical distance it occupies in the overall landscape setting. Because of its flatness, it will more than likely be only a sliver in the total scene. We all have a deep psychological connection with water, and this I believe makes us try to draw it larger than it actually is.

Textures can run vertically if you will take the time to get the "feeling" flat. These verticals symbolize reflections, and are especially good when the surface is quiet and still.

Water and a mirror are identical.

The second factor concerning water is that the textural indications should run horizontally, following the rule of textural perspective referred to in an earlier chapter. Unlike grass, however, you will want to take more liberties with water in order to catch the shimmer of light and the effects of even a slight breeze.

The third factor has to do with reflections. Understanding how reflections work is relatively simple. Begin by holding a small mirror out in front of your drawing pad. Study it, then draw what you see.

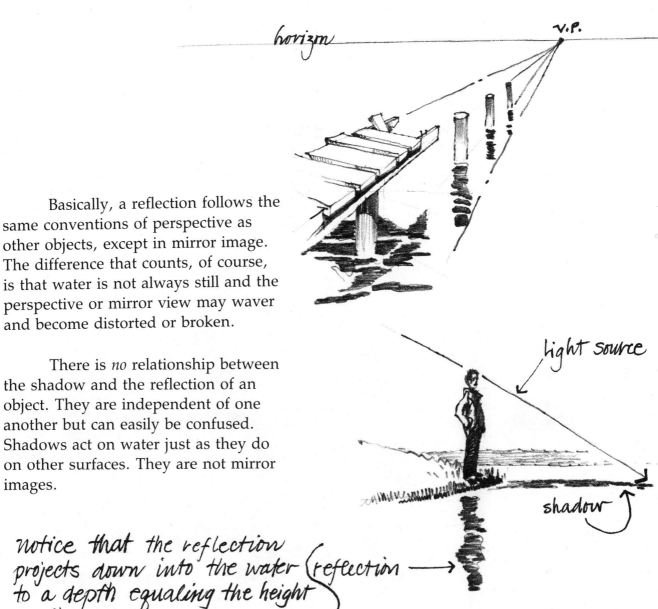

Basically, a reflection follows the same conventions of perspective as other objects, except in mirror image. The difference that counts, of course, is that water is not always still and the perspective or mirror view may waver and become distorted or broken.

There is *no* relationship between the shadow and the reflection of an object. They are independent of one another but can easily be confused. Shadows act on water just as they do on other surfaces. They are not mirror images.

notice that the reflection projects down into the water (reflection →) to a depth equaling the height of the man.

The reflection appears darker than the object being reflected because water is dense and full of particles, and also because the surface below (the bottom) clouds the image.

Frank Rines. On the Cherwell, Oxford,
England, *c. 1929. Pencil. (Courtesy of Norman
Rines)*

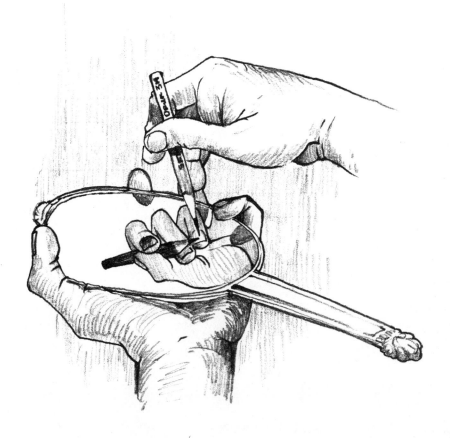

Look at your mirror again and review these final points. First, place your pencil on the mirror. Notice that if you lean the pencil to one side or the other, the reflection complements the angle. Lean the pencil forward toward you and backward away from you. What happens? The reflection will be longer than the pencil appears to be and then shorter. The view with the mirror is drawn with the pencil leaning away from you.

Drawing water will take practice and patience at first, but knowing a few facts won't hurt. For example, moving water, such as may be found in a great waterfall, generally is best illustrated by contrast—in other words, by *not* drawing it. Draw everything else and let the splash and fury of the water create itself with the white of the paper.

Drawing the things you see is okay. Eventually, however, you will need to know how things work. This knowledge frees you to invent. Having the confidence to break the tie with the things you see is based on knowing how they work.

13. Clouds

Clouds are similar to the last two study areas (land and water) in one primary way—and if you've flown very much, you will have seen this for yourself. Clouds encircle the earth in layers. These layers and individual clouds in the layers may have differences within themselves, but they all have the common characteristic of "horizontality."

Air lies in thermal layers. In summer, for example, the heated ground heats the air, and it rises upward. When the rising air contacts a cold thermal layer it vaporizes, causing a cloud. These thermal layers rotating around the earth are called winds aloft. They cause the clouds to shear and move after being formed. A thunderstorm is a dramatic realization of the process. But notice even here that the bottoms are flat, reflecting the source of their origin—the land below.

M.C. Escher. Castrovalva, *1930. Lithograph. (Courtesy of Collection Haags Gemeentemuseum, The Hague)*

There are several other sources of clouds - frontal movements, cyclonic storms, tropical depressions, etc.

cold → warm

Horizon

But the cloud forms generally follow this form: Flat bottoms and rounded tops.

The actual drawing of clouds is perhaps one of the more tricky subjects because a cloud doesn't always have a clearly defined edge. Here are a few techniques to get you started.

ascending strokes from light to dark in a form creating fashion.

after "FRESH AIR" 1878 by Winslow Homer

long sweeping horizontals that contrast the landscape.
after "The 'Round Cushion' Pine at Aoyama" c. 1823 by Hokusai

Combining long sweeps with building storm clouds and ultrahigh whisps of cirro-stratus - a popular painting technique.

after "Niagara Falls" 1820 by Alvan Fisher

Generally speaking, the higher a cloud is, the more stereotyped its form becomes. The highest clouds are usually flat, misty vapors of water and ice-like mashed cotton candy. Usually the lowest clouds are the most difficult to draw (being the least formed).

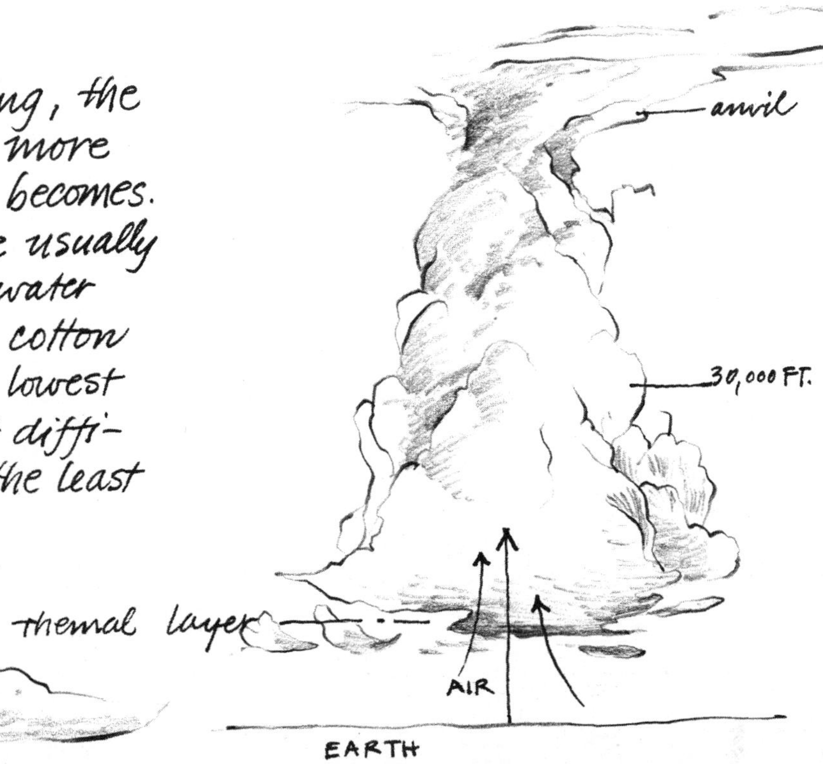

anvil

30,000 FT.

thermal layer

AIR

EARTH

The use of line quality - little rich strokes that suggest form - and a sort of reverse textural perspective can be useful.

Abstraction such as these may serve on occasion, but that best come later.

light

shadow

shade

Remember that clouds are subject to the action of light and will respond with shades and shadows. The trick here is to avoid crisp definitions while you use the same principles.

Victoria, Sicily, 1976. Ink.

14. The Sky

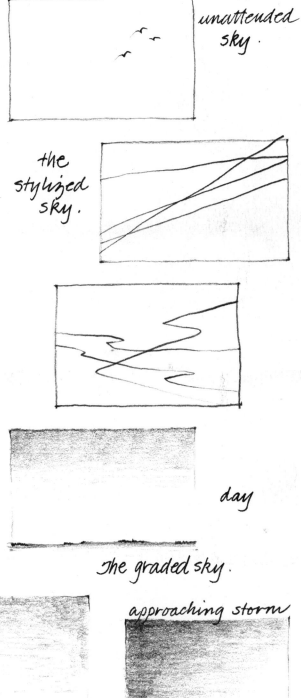

the unattended sky.

the stylized sky.

day

The graded sky.

The sky is often taken for granted but, with a few extra scratches, can be an active contribution to the drawing. It should be imagined as a great dome to be illustrated by *grading*. Grading is the gradual application of graphite from light to dark and/or vice versa. Drawing the sky as a positive part of your work can give the drawing an unequaled sense of atmosphere and space.

Leaving the sky unattended is sometimes a perfectly acceptable solution. Many depend on the viewer's eye to fill the void. However, for dramatic effect, try some illusory lines or smooth grading from top to bottom, bottom to top, sides to the middle, or from one side alone.

night

fog or haze

approaching storm

Rome

15. Architecture and Structures

Architecture and structures—buildings, bridges, monuments, and so on—occupy a central chapter in human history and are another one of the great subjects for drawing.

That in itself is a good reason to learn to draw architecture. But there is more. Lots more. The design of buildings and structures is still the most dominant design and construction activity on earth. You might remark, "But I'm no architect." If you are a designer or an artist, you can be sure that sooner or later you will have to deal with architecture and architects. The activities of man are usually housed.

As you draw a building, let's say a place of worship, you gain understanding far beyond what is on the drawing board. You begin a kinship—a kinship with the people who go there, with the myths and events that they hold sacred, with the artists and craftsmen who fashioned every detail, with the architect and the engineer, and finally with the setting.

The drawing of bridges will teach you worlds about engineering. The drawing of barns and docks and factories will teach you about farming and shipping and manufacturing. The drawing of architecture and structures will tune your awareness of the man-made world.

Via Giacomo Medici, Rome, 1975. Ball-point pen.

Spanish baroque, Sicily, 1976. Pencil.

Khajuvaho, India, 1976. Ink.

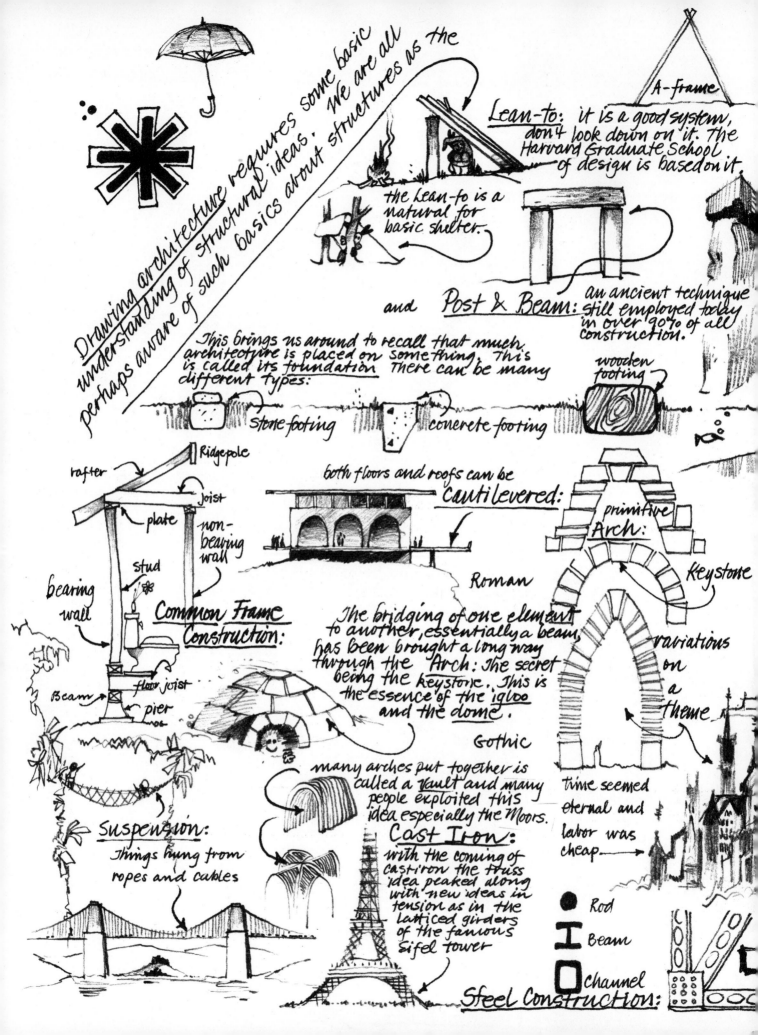

Drawing architecture requires some basic understanding of structural ideas. We are all perhaps aware of such basics about structures as the

A-frame

Lean-to: it is a good system, don't look down on it. The Harvard Graduate School of design is based on it.

the Lean-to is a natural for basic shelter.

and Post & Beam: An ancient technique still employed today in over 90% of all construction.

This brings us around to recall that much architecture is placed on something. This is called its foundation. There can be many different types:

wooden footing

stone footing   concrete footing

Ridgepole

rafter

joist

plate

non-bearing wall

stud

bearing wall

Common Frame Construction:

Both floors and roofs can be Cantilevered:

primitive Arch:

Keystone

Roman

variations on a theme

Beam

floor joist

pier

The bridging of one element to another, essentially a beam, has been brought a long way through the Arch: The secret being the keystone. This is the essence of the igloo and the dome.

Gothic

time seemed eternal and labor was cheap.

Suspension: Things hung from ropes and cables

many arches put together is called a vault and many people exploited this idea especially the Moors.

Cast Iron: with the coming of cast iron the truss idea peaked along with new ideas in tension as in the latticed girders of the famous Sifel tower

Rod

Beam

channel

Steel Construction:

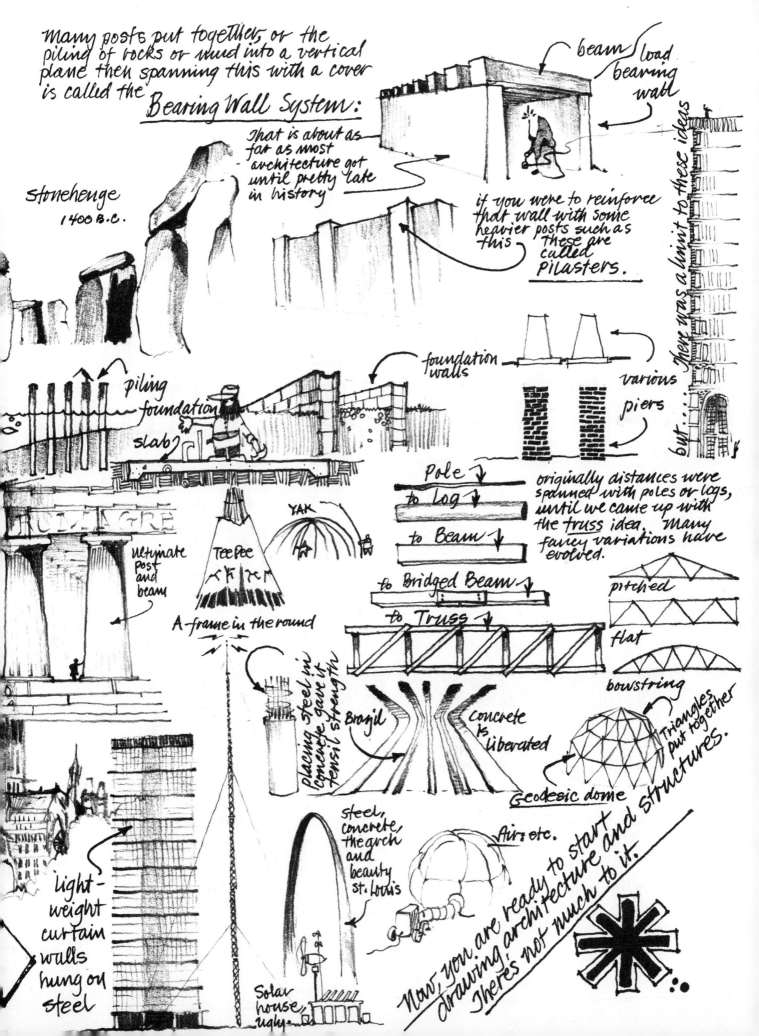

Many posts put together, or the piling of rocks or wood into a vertical plane then spanning this with a cover is called the **Bearing Wall System:**

beam — load bearing wall

That is about as far as most architecture got until pretty late in history

stonehenge 1400 B.C.

if you were to reinforce that wall with some heavier posts such as this these are called **Pilasters.**

but... there was a limit to these ideas

piling foundation slab

foundation walls

various piers

originally distances were spanned with poles or logs, until we came up with the truss idea. Many fancy variations have evolved.

Pole to Log to Beam

ultimate post and beam

TeePee
A-frame in the round

YAK

to Bridged Beam
to Truss

pitched
flat
bowstring

Triangles put together structures.

Placing steel in concrete gave it tensil strength

Brazil

concrete is liberated

Geodesic dome

light-weight curtain walls hung on steel

steel, concrete, the arch and beauty St. Louis

Air, etc.

Now, you are ready to start and drawing architecture and structures. There's not much to it.

Solar house, ugly.

Drawing architecture will require that you take time out to study materials. A good way to begin this study would be to return to the warm-up exercises that you've been doing right along. Lay out a series of boxes within which you can practice. Get some examples of materials: bricks, stones, blocks, boards, poles, posts, logs, cables, pipes, gravel, sand, tile, glass, shingles, tin, nails, rivets, girders, lattice, and so on. Draw these things until you have some suitable symbolic way to represent them. For the time being, just concentrate on materials. Go sit by a wall and draw the parts that make it up.

First, study materials carefully.

Louvre, Paris, 1976. Ball-point pen.

ARCHITECTURE AND STRUCTURES **137**

If you are still saying, "I can't even draw a straight line," then you're in the right place. Drawing architecture relies on the developing skill of drawing straight lines without the use of straightedges (rules, triangles, bars, etc.). So here's how you do it. The first and best way is to look at the line you are about to draw. Imagine it there on your paper. Then with a definitive stroke (sort of akin to slicing a watermelon) cut the line onto the paper. Curl your brow, cock one eyelid up to the side, grit your teeth, and draw it!

Now you do it. Thirteen straight vertical lines. Let's go.

1   2   3   4   5   6   7   8   9   10   11   12   13

Old wall, Siena, 1975. Felt pen.

Don't worry if you miss the preliminary line at first. Try some short ones, then slowly increase the length.

Another normal and perfectly acceptable method for drawing a straight line is to precede it with a very light preliminary line. Try this method then; score a light preliminary line then directly on top of that place the finished line. Do one in between each of these.

Remember that the hand and arm are basically on a circular system that revolves around your shoulder. This makes drawing straight lines difficult. It is not a natural move- ment. The hand and arm must make complex adjustments as you go along. Be patient. Involve the rest of your upper torso if you can. Try adding a bit of stiffness to the whole upper part of your body. Don't place all the responsibility for that straight line on your hand.

natural radius

fixed point

Try a series of horizontals with these thoughts in mind.

Here is an approach for drawing the straight line that allows you to study it as you go. Draw the line with short, regular strokes that, added together, make up the single line.

you can watch your progress

note that these lines are done rapidly. Do not study each movement. Keep your destination in mind.

Practice this approach both vertically and horizontally.

Many hours of practice will be necessary to master the straight line. If you are having trouble, do a preliminary line very lightly, then try following that with a series of rapid short dashes. Also, you should consider playing around with cubes. These little boxes can greatly aid your control of lines. Fill pages with them.

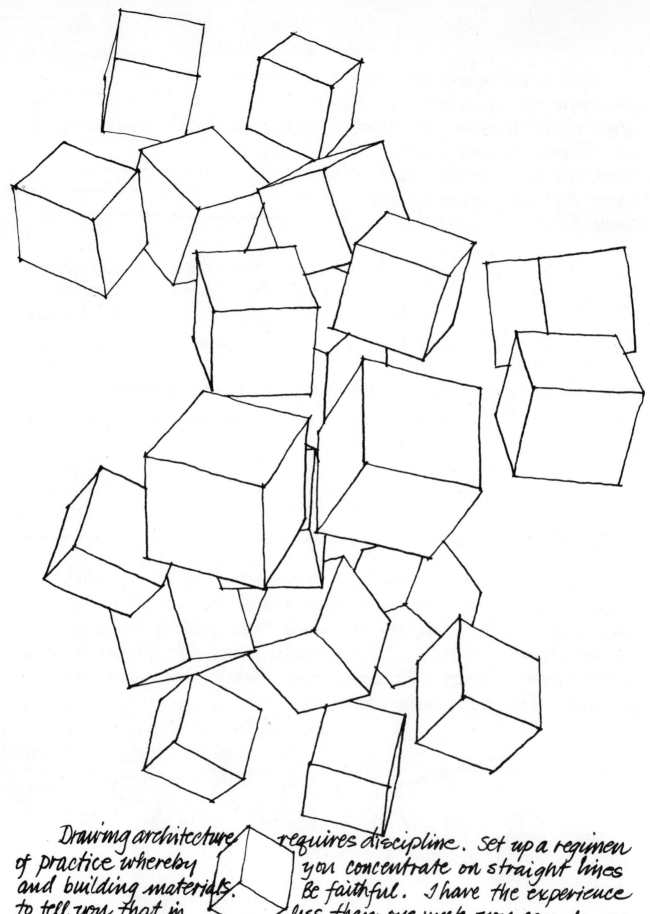

Drawing architecture requires discipline. Set up a regimen of practice whereby you concentrate on straight lines and building materials. Be faithful. I have the experience to tell you that in less than one week you can demonstrate remarkable progress. Begin by rendering this page.

As you begin your studies of materials, draw them as you find them. In other words, in perspective. We will discuss this in more detail later, but for now draw what you see. Try to notice the way materials vanish away from you.

Roman garden, 1975. Felt pen.

I don't want to alarm you, but if you have struggled along this far, and you're still hanging in there, it is only fair to tell you that drawing architecture gets considerably more precise. Buildings are the second most complex subject you can tackle, the first being people. Notice that we haven't talked much about them either. Thus far we have been dealing with things and conventions that are not too hard to grasp. The things we've drawn have simply not required exactness. Architectural drawings, even freehand ones, require a special degree of exactness.

Mark W. Smith. Soldiers, Sailors, *1974. Pencil. (Courtesy of the artist)*

Child's drawing. Marker and crayon.

Sketchbook, Italy, 1975. Mixed media.

In chapter 4 we introduced the _line weight_ convention. I haven't referred to it much since, but line weight is a big help when drawing architecture. Place the heavier lines along the edge and make them progressively smaller as the value of each element decreases. For the most part, this convention should remain fairly subtle.

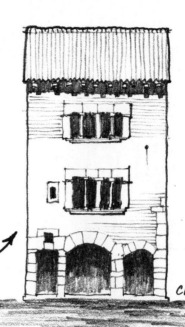

cluny

Once you have a bit of confidence about lines and materials, begin drawing architectural details: doorknobs, corners, joints, connections, embellishments, and so on.

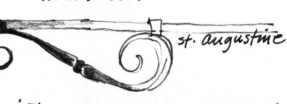

st. augustine

New England

Fill a few pages with carefully drawn details.

TWA terminal

If you are faced with drawing a detail which contains a series of repetitious elements, such as a banister, use your <u>preliminary lines</u> to assure consistancy and speed. Lay out sketchy lines that form an appropriate grid. <u>Sketch in the forms</u> and then <u>finalize</u> the drawing, using <u>line weight and an appropriate texture</u>. Don't make the mistake of trying to draw each element separately.

Note that the scheme mentioned above works for <u>perspective</u> drawings as well.

If the amount of information is unreasonably complex you must not be above simplifying it. Often the deciding factor will be time and interest. In the case of an extremely complex subject where time and/or interest is limited, abstract it and try to express its essentials. This will come with practice.

preliminary grid

preliminary layout

sketchy forms of banister

final lines & textures

layout grid

sketchy forms

finaling

v.p.

after: J. Bertelli

Ponte Vecchio, Florence, 1975. Dry felt pen.
(Courtesy of Hanna Shapiro)

16. Details and Other Observations

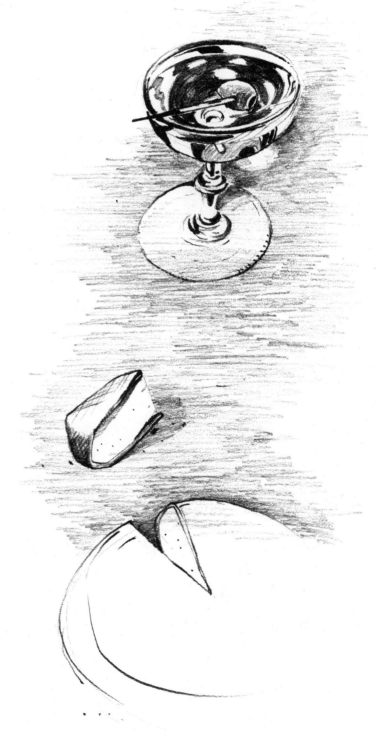

Drawing architecture is full of all sorts of learning experiences. However, may I caution that unless you make each lesson a part of your developing skill, you will be obliged to relive each experience many times. A wise sculptor once told me, "Many people go through school but few let school go through them." There is nothing wise about starting at 5000 B.C. every time you wish to express yourself. Thus these details and other observations.

Begin by speeding up. Don't fret over each and every line. In other words, don't *worry* the drawing onto the paper. The drawing of the Ponte Vecchio was completed in twelve minutes. They do not always go as quickly, but on this occasion the pen was flying. Let it fly and join in your hand's ability to move quickly. The result is very often both appropriate and attractive.

this,

Reexamine proportion. what is the proper height to width relationship?

this,

or this.

One of the very first things we discussed was _proportion_, which, as you remember, is the relative height to width of an object or space. As you begin to enlarge your drawings of architecture, you will need to carefully examine proportions.

A common error is to miscalculate the initial proportions. Use the preliminary lines to locate the building according to its proper proportions.

Begin your drawings of architecture with side views or elevations as they are called.

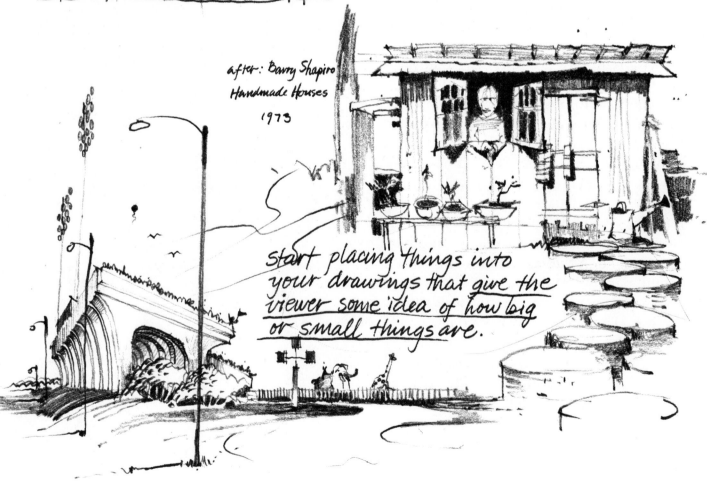

after: Barry Shapiro
Handmade Houses
1973

start placing things into your drawings that give the viewer some idea of how big or small things are.

a small but important thing to keep in mind, when drawing, and especially when drawing architecture, is to keep a good stock of sharpened pencils around. If you prefer, get one pencil with a hard lead for sketching in your preliminaries. I keep at least one dozen sharpened, soft-lead pencils around at all times.

When a wall or surface does not have a distinctive texture, such as concrete or glass, or when you wish to simplify the treatment, it may be valuable to use a *tone*. A tone, for our purposes, is the application of darkness to distinguish one surface from another. It results from the variety in the amount of light a surface reflects. All surfaces reflect some degree of tonal separation; however, the eye doesn't always pick this up. Use tones to highlight certain things you want to bring out. You have the power to avoid confusing the viewer's eye. Employ tones to your advantage. Begin now to look very closely at buildings and you will indeed see these subtle aspects.

Baltimore, Md.

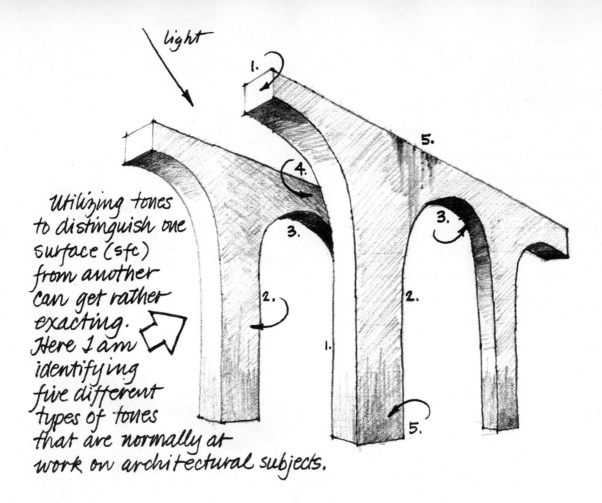

light

Utilizing tones to distinguish one surface (sfc) from another can get rather exacting. Here I am identifying five different types of tones that are normally at work on architectural subjects.

There are five basic types of tone:

1. *Little or no tones.* These surfaces are receiving full light.

2. *Even tones.* These surfaces are evenly turned away from the light.

3. *Dark tones.* These surfaces are not receiving any light.

4. *Subtle, graded tones.* These result from three things: first, there is less light in this area; second, this area is in high contrast to a fully lighted surface (no. 1); and, third, you do not want to confuse the viewer.

5. *Environmental tones.* These result from rain splash, dust, age, insects, and plant life.

There are others. For example, one type of tone is used to display reverse tonal variation on any object as it passes from sky to ground. The sky is usually clear (white). As it nears the ground it often gets cluttered and darker, and the ground is almost always dull or darker as well. By reversing the treatment of an object as it passes through these extremes, you can separate and highlight the object.

In reality this actually happens, but often we are not tuned in to these slightly less obvious qualities of the visual world.

Hagia Sophia, Istanbul, 1976. Dry felt pen.

HAGIA SOPHIA
ISTANBUL

Gianicolo, 1975. Ink.

Whereever practical, overlap one object over another. The eye, in concert with experience, has the special ability to perceive three-dimensional qualities on a two-dimensional surface. The use of overlapping elements is a reliable standby to heighten the sense of space and reality.

This brings us to the subject of *contrast*. Contrast is the technique of alternating black and white to achieve separation and distinction. But now you say, "He is repeating himself." True, but bear with me. Contrast overlaps texture and tone, but it is unique as well. Contrast is another important piece that contributes to the whole drawing. The whole drawing, as we are discovering, has many such useful if not valuable pieces.

Much of what we enjoy about architecture has to do with its contrast to the rest of the landscape. The rich modular units of texture and individual expressions of different people can be captured by paying close attention to texture.

"A great deal can be usefully taught about art, about the practice of it. But no one can teach art. The artist must find it for himself."

Pye, The Nature & Aesthetics of Design
1964

The Messa, Siena, 1975. Ink.

Now, here is a real gem. Add a few crazy dots here and there. I call them atmospheric dots. Use discretion, but

that kind of footwork can give a drawing a sense of space. It has been going on for a long time. A well-kept secret.

Also, place your emphasis along the edges and corners. A few precise strokes and textures placed just right can turn an entire wall into adobe, brick, or stone.

Yucatan.

This next tidbit is like a formula. Generally I prefer to stay clear of excess dogma, but too many drawings have demonstrated proof that irregular and uneven textural units are preferred. Sounds like an advertisement, but it's true. Mastering this trick so that it does not appear forced or contrived is not easy.

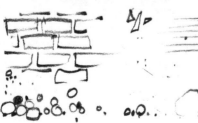

Match the size of the textural unit (logs) to the overall size of the structure. Choosing the wrong size unit can dramatically change the perceived size of the object.

Hayes Town. Castle Combe, 1977. Pencil.
(Courtesy of the artist)

Katmandu, Nepal, 1976. Ball-point pen.

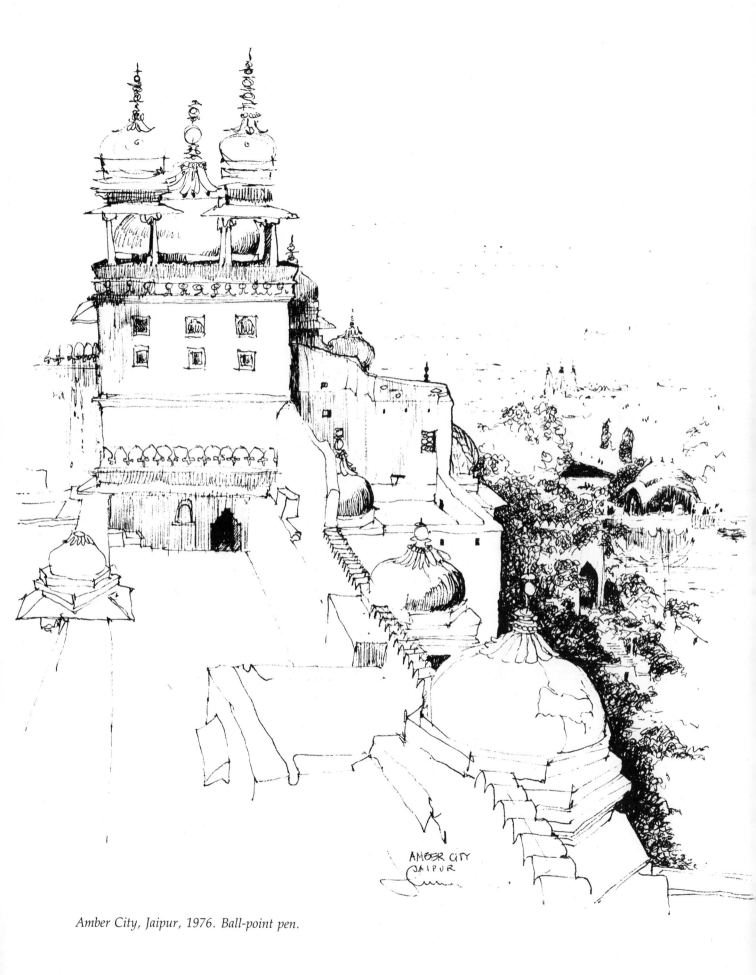

Amber City, Jaipur, 1976. Ball-point pen.

you simply score light projection lines at the coventional angle of 45°, cut them off when they adequately represent the amount of projection forward of or behind a nearby surface, and fill in the resultant areas with an appropriate shadow.

imagined light source ↙

We introduced the subject of *shade and shadows* in chapter 9. For drawing trees and other plants, shades and shadows enhance the texture and add to the fullness of the plant. For drawing architecture and structures, shades and shadows define the surfaces and give the eye specific messages about the object's three-dimensional reality. If you are in a city, among a complex of buildings, your eye will depend on shade and shadow to guide you and allow you to perceive the solid and void interplay of building, street, alley, doorway, and window. Textures are important, as are color (which is outside the scope of this study), and tones, and so on, but shade and shadow are your real allies. To illustrate buildings, shade and shadow cannot be overlooked.

There are many conventions associated with shade and shadows when drawing architecture. For example, when drawing the side view of something (window) it is customary to add shadows in an approximatioin of the amount of projection that each surface has from the wall. These shadows are usually placed to the lower right or left. Often this choice depends on what position would best demonstrate the object and not, as you might suspect, on the position of the sun.

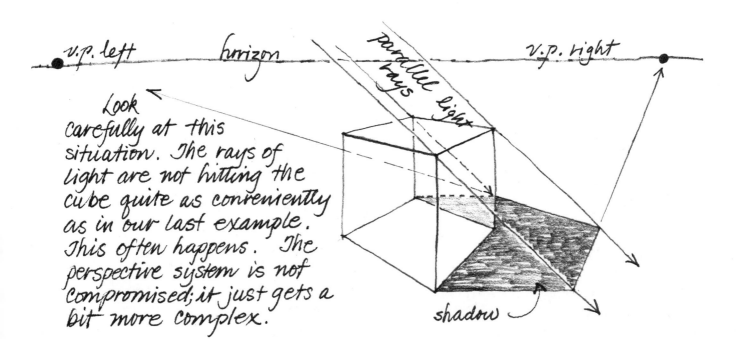

v.p. left   horizon   v.p. right

parallel light rays

Look carefully at this situation. The rays of light are not hitting the cube quite as conveniently as in our last example. This often happens. The perspective system is not compromised; it just gets a bit more complex.

shadow

v.p. left   horizon   V.P. right

Taking an aerial view of another condition, notice that the light rays are askew of the corner of the box. This creates another slightly more involved shadow. Again the perspective system is not compromised. There are many other more confounded positions that a shadow can take. But, if you understand basically how light functions and you can continue to develop your powers of observation, these few examples should serve to launch a more complete understanding.

parallel light rays

shadow

askew

DETAILS AND OTHER OBSERVATIONS   **163**

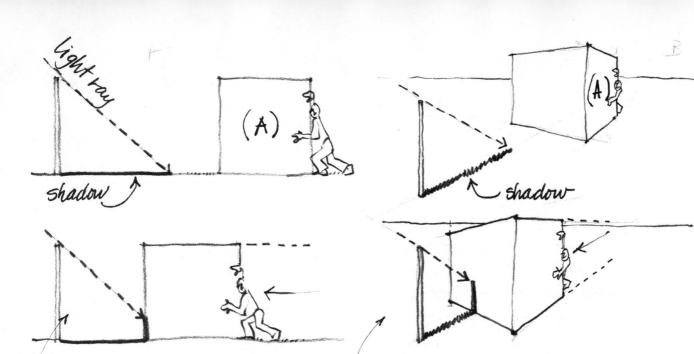

Light ray

(A)

shadow

(A)

shadow

notice how a shadow responds to an intervening object. As the cube (A) is pushed into the path of the shadow, the shadow is displaced onto the side of the cube.

Take another look at the shadow in perspective. Understanding this simple but important condition is invaluable for representing all manner of architectural subtlety.

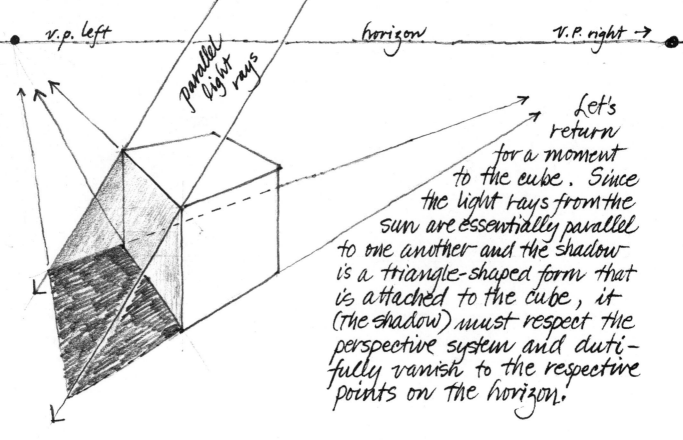

v.p. left　　　　　horizon　　　　　V.P. right →

parallel light rays

Let's return for a moment to the cube. Since the light rays from the sun are essentially parallel to one another and the shadow is a triangle-shaped form that is attached to the cube, it (the shadow) must respect the perspective system and dutifully vanish to the respective points on the horizon.

Sharestan Bridge, Iran, 1976. Fountain pen.

Bryant Park, New York City

17. More on Perspective

We would not be treating architecture fairly if we did not review the principles of perspective. The perspective system introduced in earlier chapters and the one referred to here are one and the same. There are other systems, but this is the most popular and useful as well as the least cumbersome.

Before a technical review of the system, I would like to reiterate the value of the predrawing analysis. Begin once again to carefully analyze your subject. Think about the building and ask yourself questions. What is the best view? Does the mass expose its structural integrity? What are the basic parts? Is it a delicate building, a classic building? What are its special features? Where is the entrance? From what direction will the light best complement your intentions? And so on. The final question then, and the beginning of the sketch, is how is its perspective arranged.

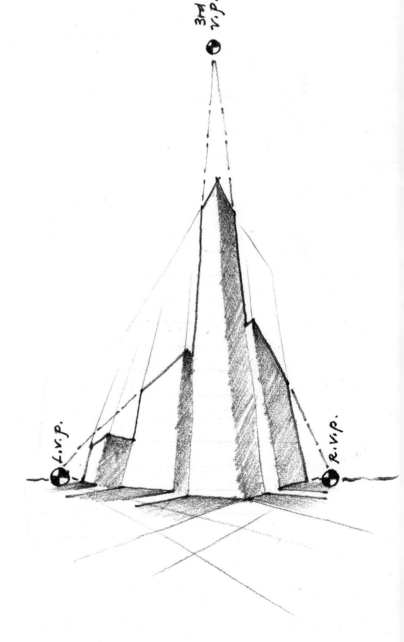

Bryant Park, New York City, 1979. Pencil.

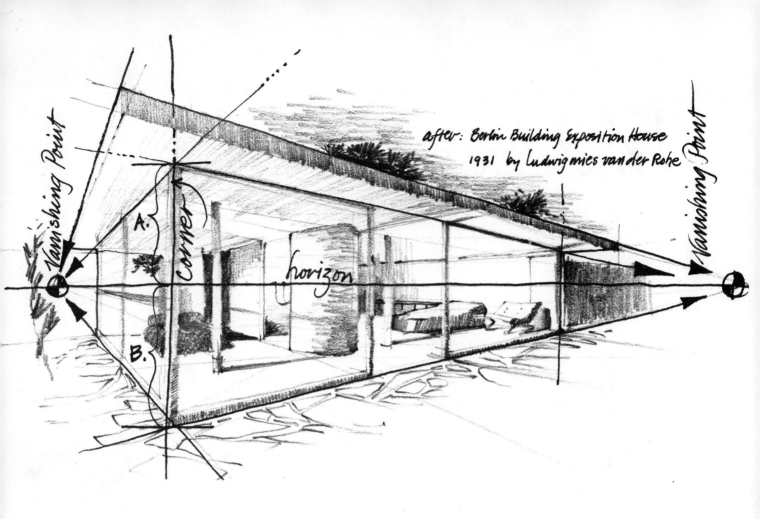

after: Berlin Building Exposition House 1931 by Ludwig mies van der Rohe

Vanishing Point

Corner

A.

B.

horizon

Vanishing Point

The perspective elements remain the same regardless of the simplicity or complexity of the subject:

1. Establish the relationship between the horizon and your eye.

2. Locate the nearest corner upon which you intend to develop the perspective layout.

3. Proportion the relative amount above and below the horizon (A and B in the drawings here).

4. Locate the vanishing points (see chapter 6).

5. Using preliminary lines, locate major and minor details of the drawing.

6. Add finishing touches.

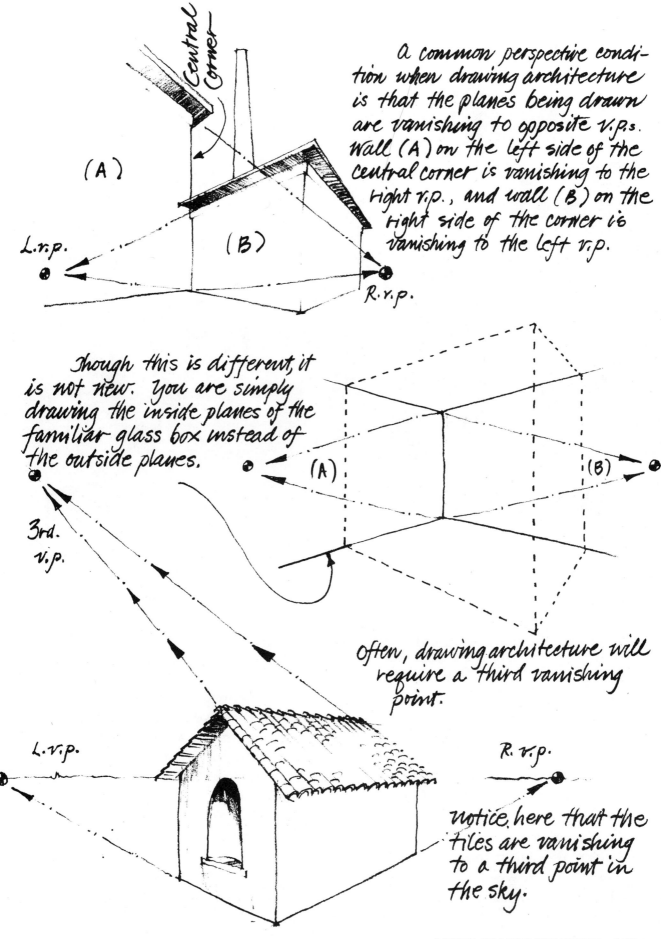

Central Corner

(A)

(B)

L.v.p.

R.v.p.

A common perspective condition when drawing architecture is that the planes being drawn are vanishing to opposite v.p.s. Wall (A) on the left side of the central corner is vanishing to the right v.p., and wall (B) on the right side of the corner is vanishing to the left v.p.

Though this is different, it is not new. You are simply drawing the inside planes of the familiar glass box instead of the outside planes.

(A)

(B)

3rd. v.p.

often, drawing architecture will require a third vanishing point.

L.v.p.

R.v.p.

Notice here that the tiles are vanishing to a third point in the sky.

John Desmond. Parlange, Louisiana, 1968.
Drafting pen. (Courtesy of the artist)

Take opportunities to practice architectural perspective by starting with simple buildings. Make the projection lines create a sketchy grid system that generally follows the mass of the subject. Lay in what minor details may be necessary. Quickly complete the sketch and go on to another subject. A week or two would be well spent on this alone.

Drawing architecture is our first comprehensive subject. By comprehensive I mean we must now include the surrounding environment. In architecture, lines and perspective must be combined with their allies, texture and light. Review the subjects covered up to this point and begin to complement the building with the enriching elements of the ground, pathways, shrubs, trees, and sky.

Baton Rouge, Louisiana

Baton Rouge, Louisiana, 1977. Pencil.

Once you've gained a bit of confidence, begin to explore and expand on the things you're learning. Search for unusual places or uncommon views. Sharpen your awarness. Investigate famous houses and abandoned mills. Draw the details and intricacies that interest you. Challenge yourself and seek criticism of your progress. What may at first appear complex is often no more than simple things put together.

Moon Valley, Kashmir, 1976. Ink. (Courtesy of Lasca Roxane White)

Luiz Sergio Santana. Embú, 1982. Felt pen.
(Courtesy of the artist)

18. *Furnishings*

The market, Italy, 1975. Ball-point pen.

There are quite a number of things that do not fit neatly into the various major study areas. One of many examples that we could provide would be the matter of furnishings. Our environment, especially the man-made environment, is filled to over-flowing with all manner of wonderful accoutrements. But don't worry—drawing these things is nothing new. You may find in fact that drawing them serves as a useful transition, and it will not only benefit you with extra practice but will add depth and sub-stance to all your work.

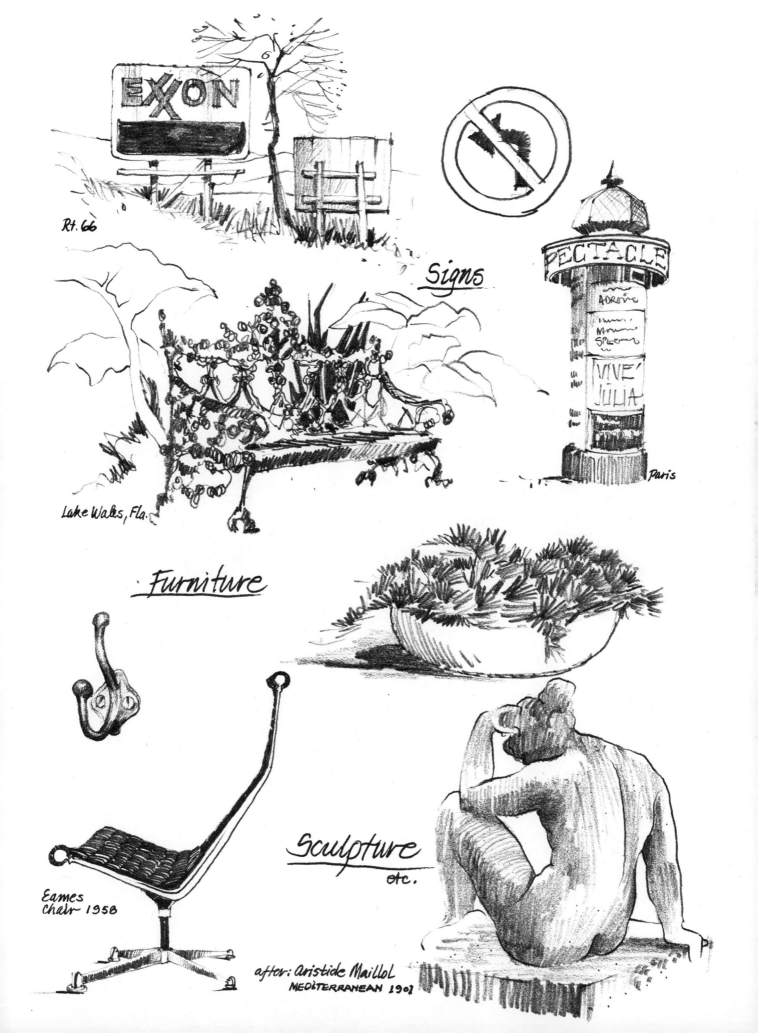

Rt. 66

Signs

PECTACLE

VIVE JULIA

Paris

Lake Wales, Fla.

Furniture

Eames
Chair 1958

Sculpture
etc.

after: Aristide Maillol
MEDITERRANEAN 1901

Degas

19. People

Perhaps nothing can raise anxieties faster than to be faced with drawing a person. Somehow drawing people stirs in us emotions over which we do not have control. Philosophers, scientists, doctors, and psychologists are continuously learning more about the grace and complexity of the human body. It is no wonder that the budding artist is so easily intimidated by such an all-encompassing phenomenon as another person. I have seen more profound feelings exchanged between an artist and a sitter in an instant than are normally available in the course of a year. Why is this? We all develop what Jung called a "complex," or a network of symbols that allows us to come to terms with the world. One of the earliest and most pervading is our image of ourselves. When we seek to symbolize ourselves (to draw), we are essentially coming to grips with this primitive complex. The symbol that results is almost never satisfying because it cannot include all

that we are. The human face, for example, is even more familiar than we know. Why? Because our concept of it is multidimensional. We see the face of a friend, but we perceive much more than his or her appearance alone. Drawing people then gets entwined with these kinds of feelings, and the artwork itself is expected to serve the seen as well as the unseen. That's a tall order, especially for a beginner. This is why we revere a great portrait. It manages to capture the unseen.

Knowing that should make it easier for you, I hope. Anyway, it's a good time to be childlike again and to trust that the things you draw are representing future potential in addition to measuring present skill. So relax, and let's learn about drawing people.

Drawing people, in a sense, is more like drawing trees than buildings. Drawing them requires fluidity and flexibility. People shift; they rock and heave; and they are often ragged and irregular. People are not fixed and static; they are loose and rounded.

Edgar Degas. Male Nude, c. 1856–58. Charcoal.

FROM BATHS IN
GREECE ROME

TOM OXLEY
ROME

SARDENIA

CORSICA

CAIRO

CORSICA

Italy, Turkey, Egypt, 1975–76. Mixed media.

The scribbles on the opposite page were done with a ball-point and fine-point ink pen. I began with the ball-point (rolls so smoothly) and ended with the ink pen. It was an exercise designed to get me into a "people mood." I would recommend, for a time at least, that you do some exercises like these. Start by twirling the pencil around without regard for any pattern. Do this for thirty seconds or so. If you like the results, develop them. Don't worry about what it means, just keep it loose and fast. Search for objects and suggestive forms and then bring them out with various levels of finish.

It has been shown that in any jumble of lines or forms the most commonly recognized objects are people. That is why we see people in clouds. Look at wood grains or tree shapes, or mountains, and so on. You see figures, noses, fingers, eyes, breasts, and a whole host of anatomical elements. Granted, you might need to stretch the imagination or stare a little harder than normal, but these things are there. Think for example about your own or someone else's childhood and how you may have been haunted by monsterlike forms that later proved to be nothing more than old rags or the shadows of trees. It is in the spirit of that kind of imagination that I would recommend that you attack these first exercises.

Start collecting drawings of people. Collect drawings, not photographs. The newspaper, for example, is full of line drawings of people (ads).

They are done by excellent fashion artists and exhibit an economy of means to capture the maximum impact. Magazines about people, sports, medicine, etc., are good sources. Build up a file of examples. I maintain a filing cabinet full of examples that I've collected over the years. Do the same for the other study areas as well. If there is one characteristic common to almost all creative people, it is that they are tireless pack rats and great collectors. It seems that just having piles of interesting junk around inspires them into action and creativity.

Trace and copy from the examples you collect. Remember, it doesn't matter *how* you gain drawing confidence; it only matters that you *do*, in fact, get it. So, by all means, trace and copy to your heart's content.

Warming up, 1968. Mixed media.

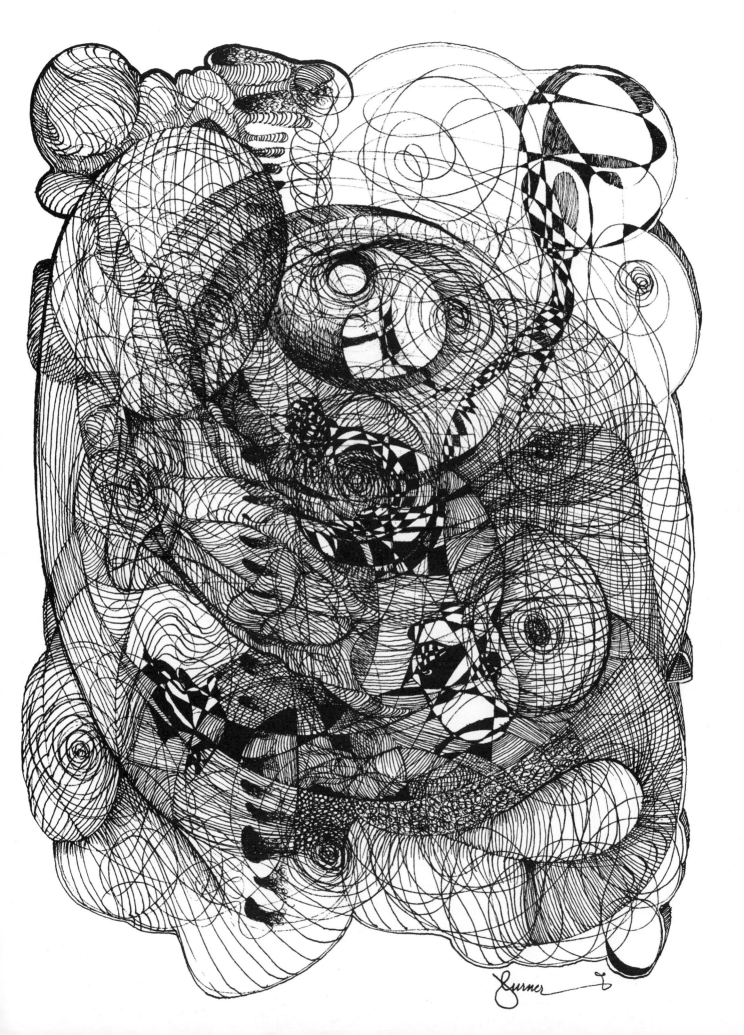

Turner

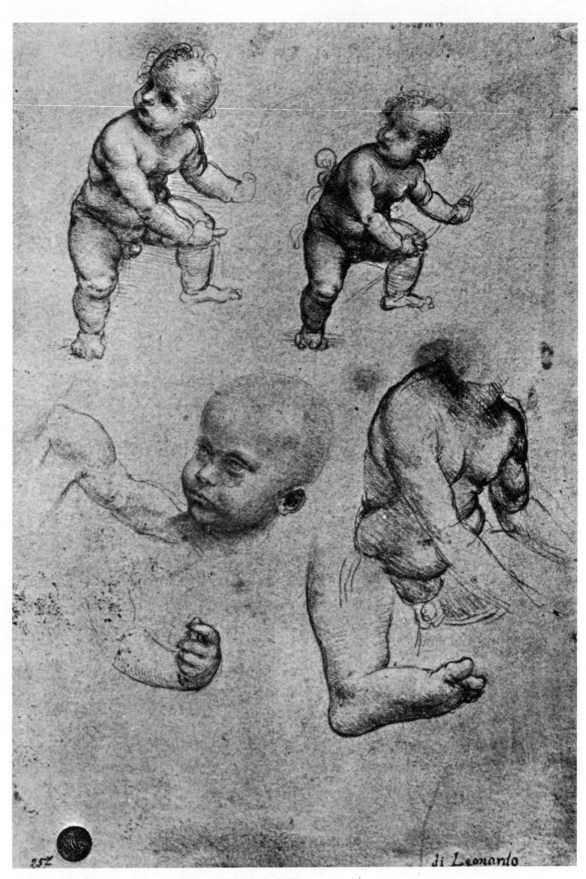

di Leonardo. Studies of a Child, *c. 1480. Red chalk.*

The head is egg shaped thus the term egghead.

eyes cut the head in half ($\frac{1}{2}$)
nose, the remaining half ($\frac{1}{4}$)
mouth, $\frac{1}{8}$ of the remaining ($\frac{1}{4}$)
Ears fill the space between the
eyes and the nose.

Front

Profile

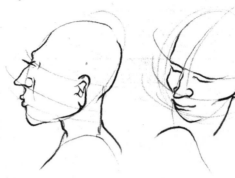

Three quarter view

Draw the egg, strike lines around the egg for the major parts and fill in the blanks.

Let's take a closer look at those individual parts.

Each individual part has its own special features. With your mirror study these elements separately.

after: J.H. Vanderpoel

Faces, Afghanistan, 1976. Mixed media.

Faces
afghanistan & India
Hurwer

The head has many beautiful attitudes. You should start drawing the head in profile and work your way around.

stress the eyes, the nostrils, and the mouth, and especially the corners.

The hair occupies at least one-third and more often up to one-half of the head.

Line Quality is of special significance when drawing people. We are all round — some more round than they'd like to be. A line placed on a two-dimensional surface is all we have to transmit this roundness. The character and quality of the line is critical.

We love how we look. That is a good reason to learn to draw people. Almost nothing interests us as much as ourselves. Witness those periods in history when we proclaimed our divinity (the ancient Greeks, the Renaissance). Whenever we get to thinking we are godlike, it seems to bring out the best: great painting, great sculpture, great architecture.

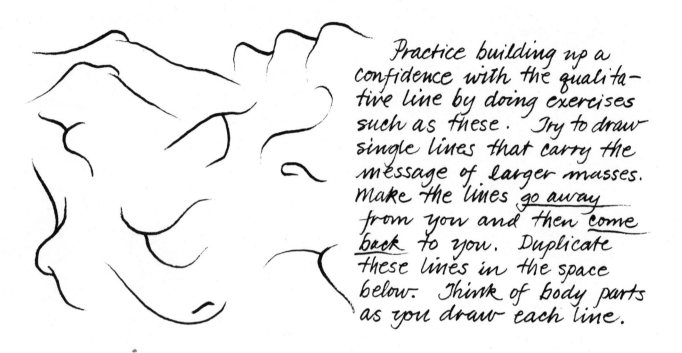

Practice building up a confidence with the qualitative line by doing exercises such as these. Try to draw single lines that carry the message of larger masses. Make the lines go away from you and then come back to you. Duplicate these lines in the space below. Think of body parts as you draw each line.

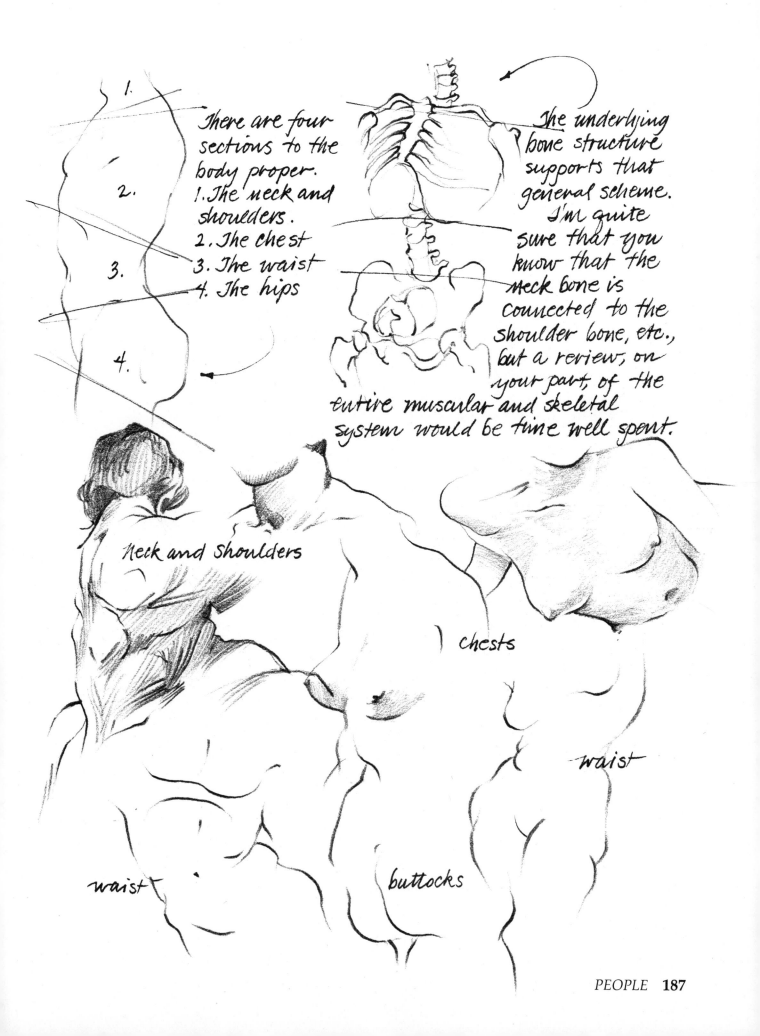

There are four
sections to the
body proper.
1. The neck and
shoulders.
2. The chest
3. The waist
4. The hips

The underlying
bone structure
supports that
general scheme.
I'm quite
sure that you
know that the
neck bone is
connected to the
shoulder bone, etc.,
but a review, on
your part, of the
entire muscular and skeletal
system would be time well spent.

neck and Shoulders

chests

waist

waist

buttocks

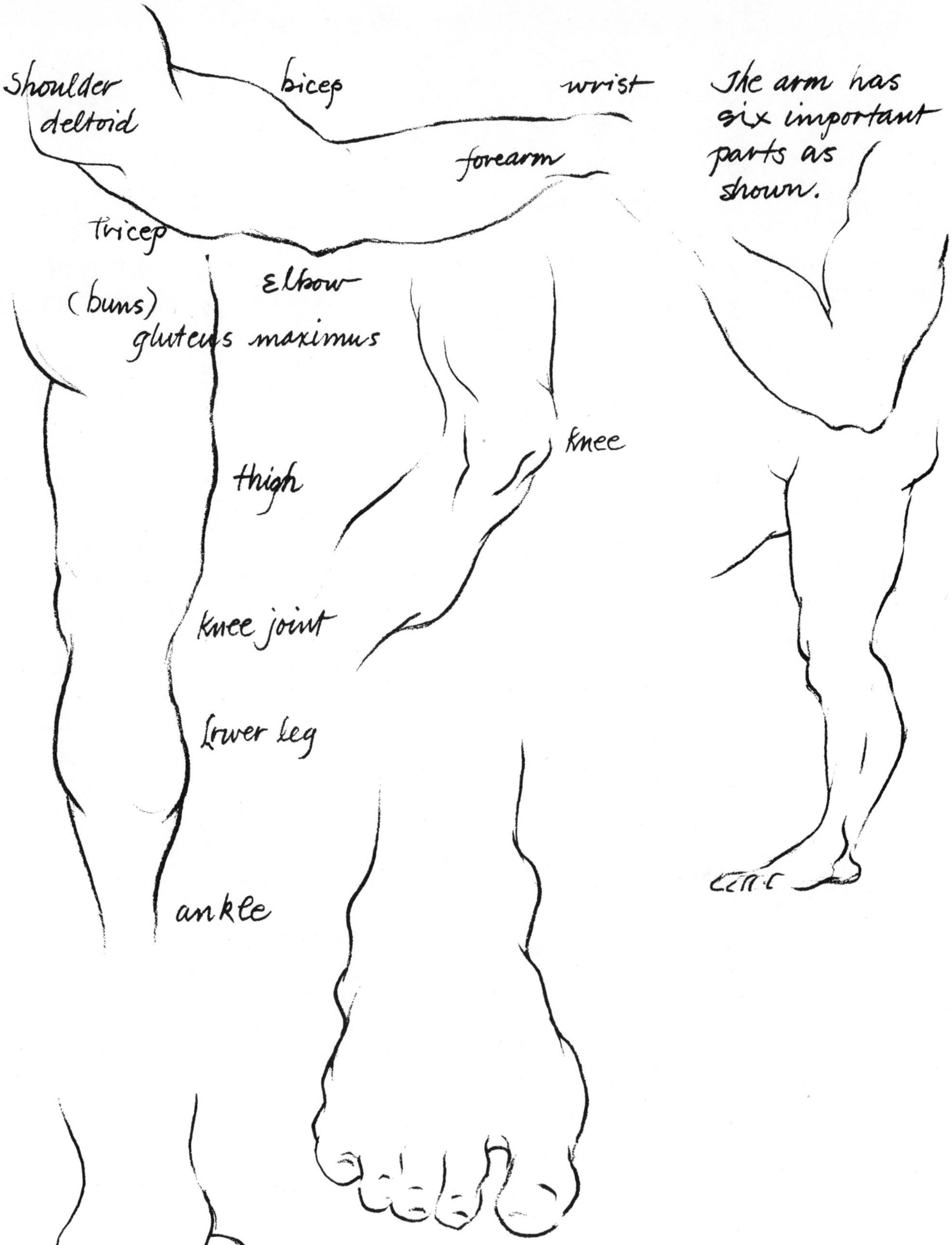

shoulder
deltoid

bicep

wrist

forearm

The arm has
six important
parts as
shown.

tricep

Elbow

(buns)
gluteus maximus

knee

thigh

knee joint

Lower leg

ankle

Hands have two major parts, the fingers opposed to a thumb.

To start with think of the hand as if it were a mitten or a boxing glove.

Then go back and look at each individual finger. Study them. Draw each one carefully.

The hand also has many graceful attitudes.

Draw your own hand many times. Try to capture such conditions as tension and rest.

Hands, 1970. Pencil.

On a serious note, drawing people requires a new level of sophistication because it brings into play all the things we've touched on—proportion, line control, perspective, texture, light, shade, shadow, symbolic representation, contrast, tone, and the refinements of line quality. Add to this the special feelings and emotions associated with the subject and you can see that things really begin to get more responsible. It is difficult to be definitive about what works well in all cases. There are fewer rules. There is overlap and trade-off from one area to the next. You will have to discriminate and judge for yourself.

One exciting and truly sophisticated subtlety that you can start practicing has to do with looking and drawing down into your paper. Place some studies deep into the fiber and fog of the paper. Start drawing as if the paper were a mist. Look at Rembrandt's *A Sleeping Child*. She isn't on the surface of the paper.

Rembrandt. A Sleeping Girl, *1630. Pen and brush in bistre.*

20. The Figure

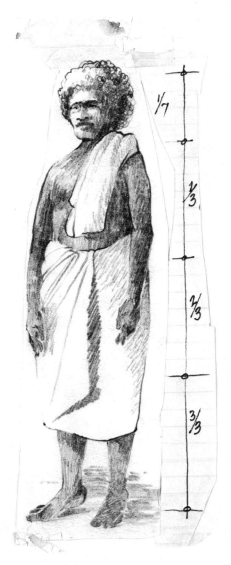

Fashion figures are often drawn 8-10 heads high to attract the customer's want to associate with tall, slim women and men.

The elbow area widest part.

The hands reach to mid-thigh

A few pointers: the head is usually one-seventh the size of the body; shoulders are two heads wide, plus or minus; below the chin the body divides into three parts (chin to navel, navel to knee, knee to toe).

Georges Seurat. Nude, *c. 1883. Charcoal on paper.*

Fiji

As you know, people come in all shapes and sizes. Don't get attached to ideal models and lose touch with reality.

Meriget, 1975. Dry felt pen.

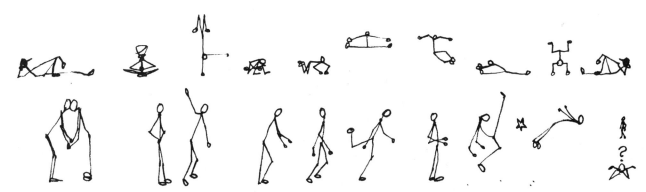

Stick figure action diagrams are excellent tools to start grasping gestures and movement. Tell stories and make up jokes with these old stand-bys.

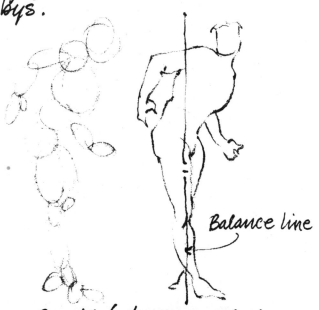

Balance line

An old but very useful process for drawing the figure is to make circles representing each major part.

after: G.B. Bridgeman

Imagine a pile of boxes that represent the parts, then fill in and mold the body around them.

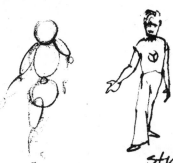

Begin these figure studies with simple postures.

Try your hand at gesture studies with light flowing lines.

Imagine the body as a pile of cans or a puppet. Strive for some movement and action.

women's shoulders and their hips are usually the same size.

men's shoulders are more often wider than their hips.

with arms out-stretched people are as wide they are tall.

Placing shadows on limbs farthest away from the viewer is a common technique to establish depth.

older folks tend to sag.

Children's heads are proportionately larger.

One of the real secrets of drawing believable people is to present them _naturally._ The fact is that most of us are a little funny looking. We don't like to practice stiff and unnatural positions. So, we _slump,_

we _sprawl out,_

and even lying down we manage to stay _off center._

and we _slouch,_

and we _lean,_

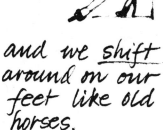

and we _shift_ around on our feet like old horses.

The point is that people are almost always asymmetrical. One side of the body is in a different position than the other.

after: Donatello, 1432.

When we sit we either _fold up_ or

This _naturalness_ was first exploited by the Greeks by 400 B.C. and remains, even today, the most popular attitude in art.

The word *scale* has to do with the relative dimension of things. In drawing, the word *scale* means the relative dimension of things to the human body. Placing people in drawings immediately establishes the size of the objects in the picture. There are other key elements that you should begin to manipulate to create scale. Think of the things we use to size up what's before us. I am always calling on common, ordinary objects to give my drawings a sense of scale—birds, plants, window panes, stones, grasses, etc. But people are the best.

Drawing people helps us (artists, designers, et al) keep in touch. That is, we need to be reminded of our clients, so to speak. Knowing *how* to draw people increases the likelihood that you *will* draw them, and this in turn helps you to keep in touch with their needs.

These two bricks are the same size

Notice how the same size lamp post changes its scale dramatically by simply adding a figure.

Scale: size related to the human body

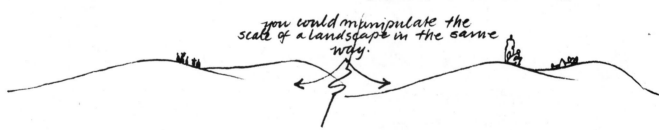

you would manipulate the scale of a landscape in the same way.

People add a magic ingredient to drawings. Drawings wake up; there is a vitality about the place. One can see, understand, and appreciate what's going on.

Kabul, Afghanistan, 1976.
Red ball-point pen.

21. People and Perspective

Lake edge. Pencil. (Courtesy of Johnson, Johnson & Roy, Landscape Architects)

after: michelangelo

Perspective is at work on individual people just as it is on other objects. The different parts of the body get smaller with distance from the eye. Setting up or imagining a perspective scheme, especially on large or near figures, is helpful in establishing the sense of three-dimensional reality.

In the larger context of perspective, the height of people can be determined by making a comparison to other objects.

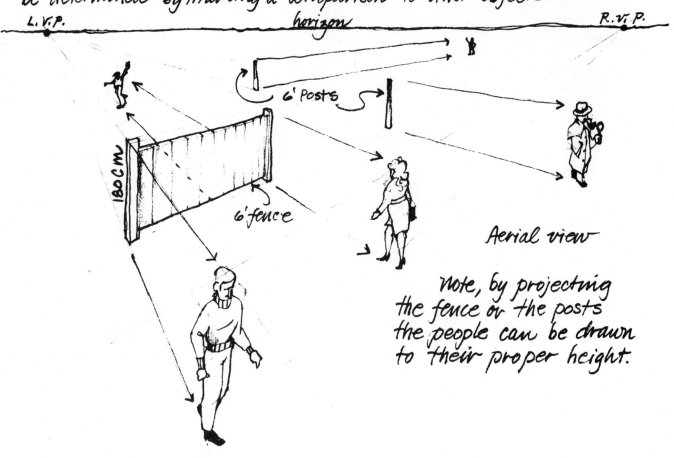

L.V.P.   horizon   R.V.P.

6' posts

6' fence

180 cm

Aerial view

Note, by projecting the fence or the posts the people can be drawn to their proper height.

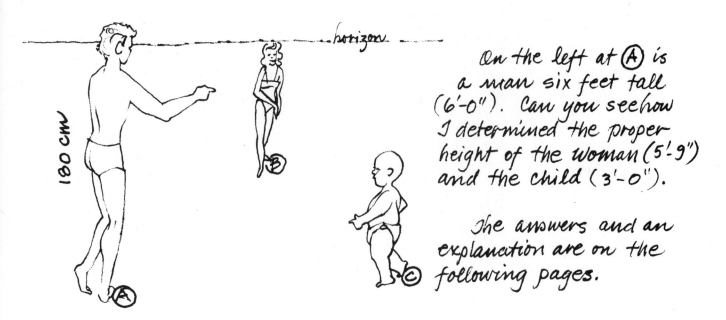

horizon

180 cm

On the left at Ⓐ is a man six feet tall (6'-0"). Can you see how I determined the proper height of the woman (5'-9") and the child (3'-0").

The answers and an explanation are on the following pages.

Here is a way to solve the perspective problem from the previous page. Draw line 1 from A through B to the horizon. Draw line 2 from the top of the man's head to the right vanishing point. This creates a 6'0" tall plane all the way to the horizon. The 5'9" woman would therefore be only a few inches below this plane. Draw a vertical line at B. Draw line 3 from C through B to the horizon. The vertical intersects with line 2 at X. From the left vanishing point, draw a line 4 through X until it passes over the child's head. Half of the distance thus created is 3'.

Here is another answer. The man is 6' tall; therefore, at any point B on the ground, the distance from that point to the horizon is approximately 5'9". The child is half as tall as the man; therefore, at any point C, the child would rise half the distance to the top of the man's head at that point.

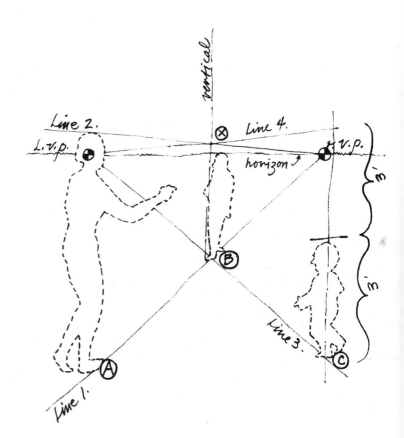

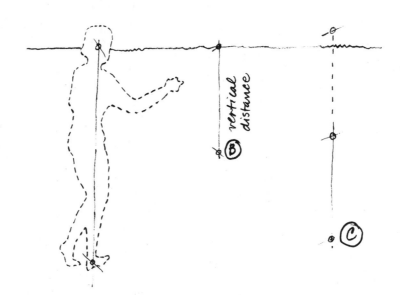

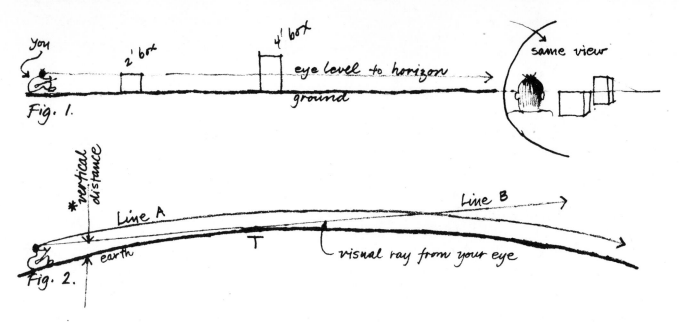

Fig. 1.

Fig. 2.

When you look out over the curved surface of the earth your vision does not flow in a curved line (line A), but rather it flows in a straight line (line B), and the horizon stops the visual ray at the tangent (T) of line B and the curve of the earth. If your eye is 3′ off the ground, this distance would be 2.28 miles:

$$\text{distance} = 1.317 \times \sqrt{\text{height of the eye}}$$

If your eye were 5′6″ off the ground (normal eye level while standing), the distance would be 3.09 miles, and if you were 1,000′ up in the Empire State Building, the distance would be 41.6 miles. Since the actual horizontal distance is so great, the eye cannot detect the subtle change of the vertical distance (*) from line B to the ground. Thus it is assumed that the vertical distance is constant, this being determined by the height of the eye (line A). Remember too that the perspective system assumes that the earth is flat, Figure 1. Crazy system, huh? But it's the best we've got. Notice that when your eye height and the horizon intersect with any object before you, you can judge its height. It is a wonderful trick and a great drawing tool.

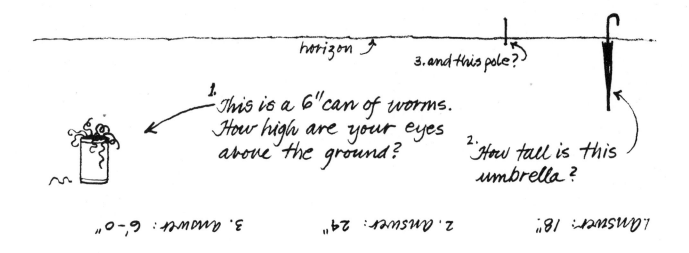

horizon →

3. and this pole?

1. This is a 6″ can of worms. How high are your eyes above the ground?

2. How tall is this umbrella?

3. answer: 6′-0″   2. answer: 24″   1. answer: 18″

Il Campo, Siena, 1975. Ball-point pen.

Part II

The Finished Sketch

September prairie, 1982. Felt pen.

22. Why Draw?

Roger Baldwin, founder of the American Civil Liberties Union, once said, "I think that fear is one of those emotions that grows out of a lack of self-confidence." Mr. Baldwin's organization has defended just about every form of scoundrel and saint there is. He was certainly not short on confidence. One reason that he did not have fear is simply that he believed that he was doing the right thing. Once you have made up your mind that you are at least trying to do the right thing, fear vanishes.

The question is, why learn to draw? That's a loaded question. We have taken quite a long look at it in the chapters so far, and I'm inclined to subtotal several noteworthy answers:

C. G. Jung wrote in *Memories, Dreams, and Reflections,* "Out of sheer envy we are obliged to smile at the Indians' naiveté and to plume ourselves on our cleverness; for otherwise we would discover how impoverished and down at the heels we are. Knowledge does not enrich us; it removes us more and more from the mythic world in which we were once at home by right of birth." The systems that take away these rights, usually by the age of twelve, need to be seriously reviewed. To draw is such a right. It is a symbolic mechanism of human expression that is embedded in us all. It is simply a natural thing to do, like speaking, writing, loving, dancing, and merrymaking.

William Morris, English poet, artist, philosopher, and exquisite craftsman, demanded a knowledge of drawing as the basis of all manual arts and as an essential element of a general education. That idea is revolutionary today only because we have drifted so far from our native skills. Almost without exception, all art is essentially manual. It is the hand in harmony with the mind. Words do not substitute for this relationship. Artists, not only in painting and sculpture, but in acting and music, in gardening, and homebuilding and in the crafts, have long known of the harmony of mind and hand. Not one or the other, but both.

Speaking of skills, the acquisition of a skill, especially in the arts, is an aid in the development of another fundamental human itch—to have taste. What is taste? Taste is a cultivated inclination toward quality. Now, that may not sound altogether sufficient in light of our typical demand for rhetorical clarity, but you must remember that regardless of interpretations, such things as taste do exist and are desirable. Indeed taste is often desired enviously, even longed for. Particularly, as you might guess, by those who don't have it. Anyway, taste is intrinsically tied up with many of the things that we hold in the highest regard—things like sincerity, honesty, appropriateness, and beauty. As with most things that we cherish and honor, there is little agreement on what constitutes an adequate definition. I do know, however, that taste can be acquired through the development of various skills. Taste is a gift from skill and experience, a delightful coincidence. Almost no activity of which I am aware is more effective in developing the desirable characteristic of taste than exercising your native abilities in an art form.

In Italian there is a term *causa sui*. It translates literally into "your cause." Ernest Becker, the great Canadian philosopher, spoke of this often. It has to do with purpose. You have a purpose if for no other reason than to deny a few important existential paradoxes. The historical accounts and the products produced by creative men and women is evidence of how beautiful a *causa sui* can be. You have at this very moment a *causa sui*, and what is more you have had it for quite a while. This is not to say that you understand it or that you are even aware of it, but it is operating. That is simply a fact. In a sense you will continue with it until you, or the force of circumstance, decides to alter or change it. Your purpose/cause may be operating unconsciously. On the other hand, it may be known to you. At any rate, it is a dynamic human component. It is realized, made conscious, when you can take pleasure in your work, when the work is of itself life-giving. For whatever reason, drawing can become a part of your purpose as easily as any craft, hobby, or vocation, and that is another reason to draw.

The mystery that may now surround a worthy cause is knowable. Our example is freehand drawing. The mystery that may now surround a cause that includes drawing as a component of your will is knowable. You can do anything you choose. That too is simply a fact. Behind this choice, then, lies purpose. And what is behind purpose? Nothing! Purpose is itself. You learn how to draw to learn how to draw. Everything else is a consequence. Even beauty, though we may quiver at its sacredness, is a consequence of purpose. As David Pye wrote in *The Nature and Aesthetics of Design:* "No one can be taught what beauty is: everyone finds that out for himself: but he can be taught what are promising places in which to look for it; and taste, as often as not, is what teaches him that."

Luiz Sergio Santana.
Roberto's Garden, 1982.
Felt pen. (Courtesy of the artist)

But what company you keep when obliging so illusive a friend as beauty, quality, taste, and great craft! Behind such choices as these (to learn to do), there are many things that will support your purpose. One of them, a big one, is your confidence. The practice of, the struggle to know a thing, brings to you, through confidence, the support that your *causa sui* needs in order to prevail. Almost nothing else is more important. No resource is so without threat to its depletion as your confidence once found.

There are those, and many I would add, that draw in order to share their work with others. This book is obviously an example of my own desire to do exactly that. Drawing brings a degree of economic security for some and certainly the praise and attention paid to the work are critical to its creator. There is a final reason, though, to clear the air and encourage your diligent efforts: drawing is a lot of fun. The sheer personal pleasure of drawing is in summary the real reason to do it.

SEA WALL OF ALEXANDRIA

23. Trying Your Wings

Part 1 was a rather vigorous program. You were exposed to a good cross section of elements: people, architecture, plants, and so on—sort of the building blocks of a finished sketch. Folded between these building blocks was a measure of theory about how and why we draw. We went over a few principles and a number of elements, after a fashion, that is, not dwelling on the pontifical nature of these aids: proportion, line, tone, texture, etc. We got lots of good, old-fashioned practice. The procedure has been somewhat classically pedagogical. I introduced a subject, laid the ground rules, kept things in a semblance of context, gave examples, demonstrated tricks, and so on. And you, in turn, vacillating with anguish from crisis to disaster, have been struggling with the development of your drawing confidence. This is good. You know that drawing can be tough; you know what a kick it is to get it right, and you know the commitment it takes to improve. Some of us got better at drawing. I know that I did. Some of us stayed about the same, but to our credit I would venture to say that none of us got any worse. Let's change a few things.

There is a basic shift of responsibility about to take place here. It is not intended to bring on any panic, but you are now more or less in charge. Spread your wings. I'm not going to rush out of the picture, but I'm going to ask that you begin sharing the load. Here is the program. For the remainder of the book we are going to discuss the finished sketch. These sketch summaries will include all or nearly all that we have discussed so far. You are more or less on your own to start drawing, stretching, and trying your wings.

Sea wall of Alexandria, 1976. Felt pen.

The Picnic

24. *Thoughtful Ideas*

Somewhere in the process of producing a drawing, you will come to regard a peculiar and much-debated subject—the idea. It goes like this. A drawing is finally a symbol by which you express an idea. All drawings are symbols of ideas. Are all thoughts ideas? In a sense, yes. A thought is a plan, a conclusion, a recollection, a projection, a test. Regardless of the meanness or the grandeur of a thought, it inherently contains an abstraction. If this is true, then ideas are all around us. We abound with a store of ideas. Yes, but wait. For, you see, while it is true that all thoughts are ideas, it is also true that some ideas are more thoughtful.

An idea that consolidates a complex of thoughts into a theme gets to be a bit more interesting. And an idea that can capture a range of related thoughts and arrange them into a cal-

culated response certainly deserves more than passing attention. Thus in drawing we are engaged in a form of communication responsibility. The drawing is the medium by which an idea, hopefully of the order of a symbolic complex of thoughts, is presented. A drawing stands as a tangible record of an idea—thus a measure of the drawing's worth. Some ideas attract us and some repel us and some leave us rather unmoved. A drawing, being the symbol of an idea, has such power.

Now you may say that this only clouds the issue of getting a drawing completed. You could not be farther from the truth. Intuitions, feelings, sensations, and thoughts are the means by which we cope with our surroundings. A thought, for lack of a better word, would be that which is your reaction to the world. Each of these components that E. F. Schu-

The picnic, 1982. Felt pen.

macher calls the "fourth level of being" is an idea. Each thought conceives a stratagem. If you sit down to draw the scene before you, there is an expression, an idea, already at work. However mundane, however detached, an idea exists. My point is that you as the artist are working at a level of ideas that has the potential to reduce a mountain of thoughts into a single, precise, thoughtful, and beautiful symbol—the finished sketch.

Now don't get yourself worked up about this because, while it is indeed valuable, it isn't always useful. That is to say, you needn't feel that because you cannot verbalize your drawing idea all is lost. This is not the case. To be able to explain a drawing in the different and even more abstract language of words is neither easy nor always appropriate. If, on the other hand, you wish your drawings to be somehow accepted by others on grounds similar to your intentions, the idea must be accessible. This access is determined not by what you have to say but by what you have drawn. The range of your drawings is limited only by the range of your ideas.

Specific examples of ideas don't always serve because they tend to be classic and at the high point of some art epoch—Michelangelo, Vermeer, Van Gogh, Picasso, etc. However, in the spirit of teaching as I understand it, these examples can often be very valuable. Here, I've employed Gustav Klimt to present one idea. Klimt (1863–1918) was a lesser-known but central figure in the international art nouveau movement. He was not one to follow others, as his erotic paintings, done in the midst of the Victorian era, attest. He was an independent, even on a subject as parochial as a park. In *The Park*, Klimt swallows the horizon to within an inch of its life. He occupies you with the facade of the trees and the sensual carpet of leaves and flowers. He consolidates a complex of longings and associations (thoughts) into a single view of an ordinary park. It becomes extraordinary because he does not allow you to deny the earth and her riches by wandering off into an endless sky. Instead, the park is the whole thing. Probably the entire network of associations, devils, angels, imps, and cherubs are wrapped up here. When you think *park* this is an essential, a painting that manages to symbolize an idea.

Another example taken from the ranks of our contemporary artists is an idea by J. H. Aronson. Siena, the historic medieval city of Tuscany, is a walled city, woven thick with color, texture, and tradition. In the heart of the city is a great plaza (open space) called Il Campo. Life revolves around this wonderful space and around the ambitious tower at the foot of the plaza. All streets and all spirits lead to Il Campo, especially in late summer when a fierce horse race, pitting the honor of the old families of Siena against one another, is run wildly around the crowded edges of the makeshift track. Aronson has chosen to represent this city in-the-round, so

Gustav Klimt. **The Park,** *c. 1910. Oil on canvas.*
(Courtesy of The Museum of Modern Art, Gertrude
A. Mellon Fund)

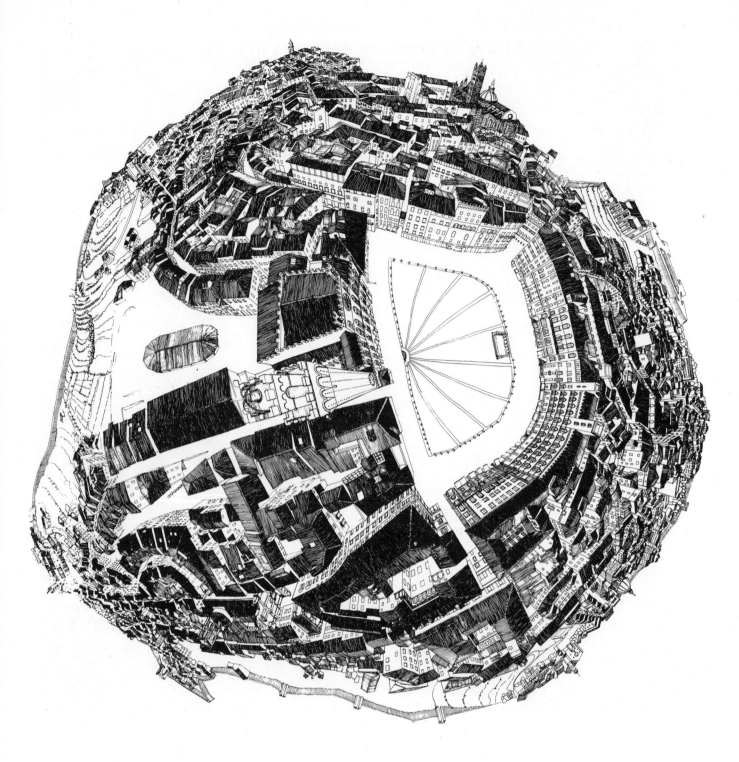

J.H. Aronson. Siena, 1972. Etching, 26" x 26".
(Courtesy of the artist)

to speak. The artist climbed to the top of the tower, seen from above at the lower edge of the plaza, and, with his camera, took a series of overlappig panoramas of the city. In his studio he reconstructed a view that could not otherwise be seen. The drawing idea was to make the city visible as if it were a planet. It is an original and appropriate idea because, for one thing, these marvelous old cities were once worlds within themselves. There was no instant news service, no instant visual record of others, and indeed many lived out their entire lives within the walls of these powerful feudal domains. Aronson captured much of that and more by exploring a thoughtful idea in his unique etching, *Siena*.

Do not be trapped nor intimidated into thinking that you only draw when you have an idea. Earlier I said "somewhere in the process" of producing a drawing you will come to regard the idea. It doesn't always come at the beginning and may wait for months, even years, to expose itself. My point is that the idea is there, waiting for you to nourish it and make it a positive part of the symbol.

25. The Finished Sketch

The problem of doing a finished sketch is in some ways the classic confrontation with design. How shall it look? There are—and I add an element of caution—a number of conventions that can help you meet this challenge. (The note of caution refers to the fact that great drawings are not great because they follow conventions.)

The first portfolio of conventions centers around the subject of *composition.* A composition is an arrangement of the parts of a drawing so that they form a whole. Those parts, besides all the things we have already covered, include a formidable list of principles and tricks to aid you in achieving the finished sketch.

This is where creativity begins to really shine. When you look out over a scene or when you are thinking about a drawing, you are beginning to compose it. Seldom will artists settle for exactly what's before them. They

manipulate it. This is a canon distinction between drawing and photography. One of the very first manipulative actions centers around *analysis.* Scratch out or mentally go over the subject. Try different approaches. Think of emotional associations, even times of day or year that might enhance the drawing. Do trial layouts.

When you actually begin to arrange things, you become involved in *balance.* You are pitting forces. Two of the primary forces are the horizontal and vertical axes.

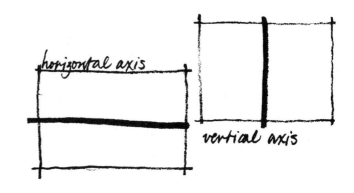

Mary Street, 1967. Graphite stick. (Courtesy of William M. Turner)

How do you know if your drawing is balanced? That isn't easy. The easiest way to achieve balance is by not taking chances. This is called *symmetrical balance.* In other words, the major pieces of drawn information center on the horizontal and vertical axes.

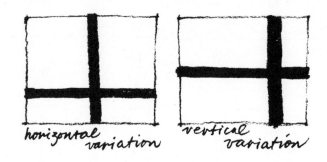

horizontal variation   vertical variation

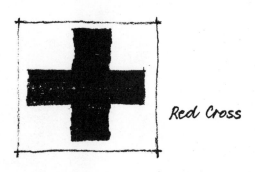

Red Cross

This kind of balance is often called formal, or the balance of opposites. In a radial sense, this kind of balance is characterized by many well-known symbols. This kind of formality is readily perceived by the viewer and leaves little for interpretation. It is said that by balancing a composition exactly, one tends to create independent parts rather than parts that contribute to a whole.

By manipulating these major axes, however, you can create variations on a theme. There is still a degree of symmetry. However, by moving one axis up or down or left or right you achieve a clearly different composition. This is mildly unsettling. Why? Because we are prone to order and symmetry. We quite naturally seek outward expression of our need for order.

"harmony" China

"happiness" Indonesia

Perfect symmetry implies stability, and unless you're careful, monotony. Thus symmetrical balance, while offering a certain assurance of perfection and order, suffers the undesirable consequence of possible boredom. It is almost always to your advantage to create some sort of variation on the theme of absolute symmetrical balance.

Shrinagar, Kashmir, 1976. Brown ink.

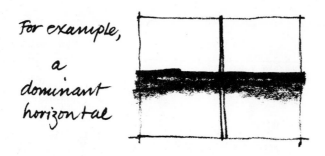

For example, a dominant horizontal

The second, and most common-ly used, method of balance is called *occult* or *felt balance*. That is, you balance unequal and irregular forces: the large with the small, the fat with the skinny, the strong with the weak, the attractive with the ugly, and so on. There are no rules with occult balance. The horizontal and vertical axes might be anywhere on the page. This form of balance requires experimentation and a willingness to be daring and adventurous.

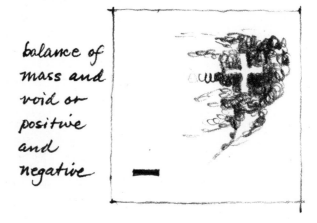

balance of mass and void or positive and negative

A slightly more abstract factor having to do with balance deals with the balance between *mass* and *void*. Begin to strike a medium between the amount of drawn information with the undrawn or negative space.

Look at your preliminary layouts. Begin to judge them. Feel them out.

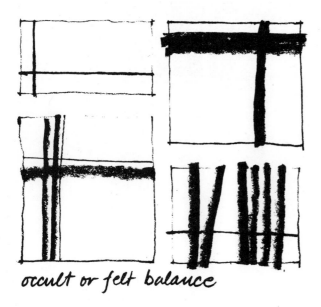

occult or felt balance

Victoria Immanuel, Rome, 1975. Drafting pen.

What constitutes the vertical or horizontal element in balance can sometimes be rather subtle. In this view of a camel on a desert, the desert edge against the sky is the horizontal axis, but the vertical axis is implied only by the camel. Balance in composition can get to be tricky and therefore exciting and interesting. There are many more atypical situations. Move toward the realm of a drawing's idea, and you may balance coarse against fine, young against old, warmth against cold, to name a few worn examples.

Occult balance may include an infinite range of other arrangements.

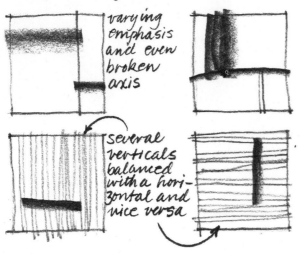

varying emphasis and even broken axis

several verticals balanced with a horizontal and vice versa

The principle of balance also has some power to elicit emotional responses. The horizontal axis is generally associated with calmness, rest, water, and earthly things. It is reassuring and stable. The horizontal suggests gravity, weight, and solidarity, while the vertical is associated with action, life, vitality, growth, daring, and even instability and threatening aspects. If you push the vertical slightly askew, you interject action, movement, drama, and even crisis.

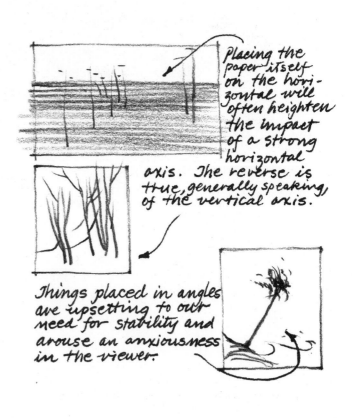

Placing the paper itself on the horizontal will often heighten the impact of a strong horizontal axis. The reverse is true, generally speaking, of the vertical axis.

Things placed in angles are upsetting to our need for stability and arouse an anxiousness in the viewer.

Balance is a dynamic and active part of drawing. Knowing how to draw is only complemented by knowing where to draw.

Santa Maria Della Salute, 1979. Felt pen.

Having something to say, being able to draw it accurately, and then getting it somehow balanced on the page doesn't always get you home free. A *focal point* or an area of *emphasis* is often an essential ingredient. You may desire the viewer to pay attention to one certain area in the sketch that is important above all else.

achieving emphasis by the manipulation of light and contrast

after: Georges de La Tour, 1645

Crisscrossing lines leading to the focal

after: Titian, 1570

As a former student pointed out, "It is not by coincidence that stars attract attention."

action directed to the focal

after: Goya, 1814

Leading the eye where you want it to go is often accomplished with lines and points of interest. There are many tricks to draw the viewer's attention to the area of interest. One technique commonly used in photography is to vary the focus or visible detail. Place the desired object/area in focus and leave the rest of the drawing out of focus. Then fade or vignette the edges.

The perspective and structural organization leading to the focal

after: Raphael, 1510

after: D'Amelio, 1964

Via Guilia, Rome, 1975. Ball-point pen.

These aids to the finished sketch should neither hamper you nor provide you with any special certainty. The truly creative artist/designer can, as Charles Eames said, "work within the creative boundaries." You need only look at the masterpieces and see that the aids used were not crutches or clichés but the ordinary, known conventions employed with discipline, craft, emotion, and genius.

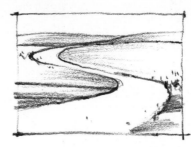

Creating an "S" curve is easier to sublimate.

Very often these leads are disguised and done repeatedly with smaller lines and elements, textures, shadows, etc. Many of the famous seascapes and landscapes are absolute virtuosos of these attractive and beckoning lines and forms.

Artists have long known ways to lead the eye of the viewer toward a desired end. There are several standbys.

The disappearing path technique is a favorite of rural landscapes, gardens, and it is often used in cartoons.

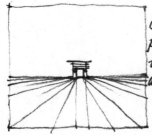

convergence by perspective is usually too obvious and boring.

progressive points of interest or things to see will generally follow an S or Z technique. see From the Rampart by Rembrandt.

Creating a "C" curve is a very common technique.

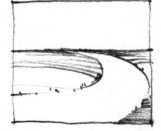

The diminution of familiar objects such as trees

Edgar Degas. Landscape in the Départment De l'Orne, *c. 1861–64. Ink and sepia wash on paper.*

Drawing the finished sketch can be compared to some aspects of set design. To design a set, the designer often tries to create an illusion of deep space within the shallow depth of the stage. One standard is to organize a series of *grounds,* as in the example on this page. Grounds are semiartificial levels of information arranged so as to create an illusion of depth. Ordinarily there should be at least three levels: *foreground,* those things used to edge or frame the view; *middleground,* those things used to establish a middle distance usually beyond and behind the foreground; and *background,* those things establishing a sense of relative distance. The sky or space will then serve as a complementary fourth ground.

In drawing you should seek to identify several grounds of information in a similar fashion. At first you should be specific and determined. Establish grounds so that there is no question of their existence. This is one of the tricks for engaging the viewer's eye. After a bit of practice, you'll find that the grounds will become second nature to you, and you'll be able to blend and disguise the overlap. Artists often include up to seven or more layers of information in order to ensure a sense of depth and space.

Value has to do with the relative lightness or darkness of an object or space. In drawing, this ranges from the white of the paper to the darkest blacks of the pencil. The scenes shown

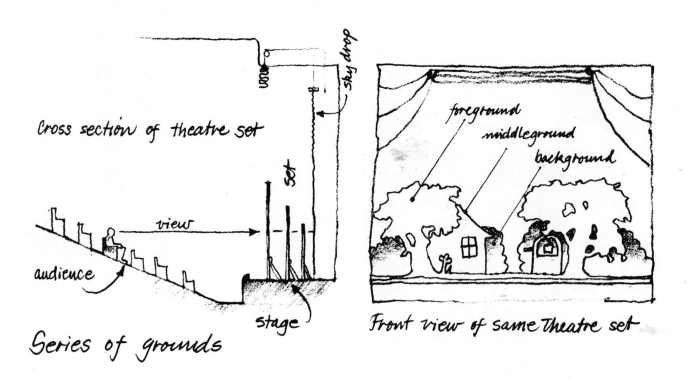

Cross section of theatre set

sky drop

set

view

audience

stage

Series of grounds

foreground

middleground

background

Front view of same theatre set

Mount Desert Island, 1979. Pencil.

1.

2.

3.

here represent the establishment of the three grounds: foreground, middleground, and background. The sky is serving as a fourth ground. You can control the picture by manipulating values from light to dark or any combination on the respective grounds. Notice that the choice of values is an overriding pencil-shading technique that is essentially at the discretion of the artist. The results are dramatically different from one approach to the next. In the first case it appears that we have a normal sunny day with the people in the shade of an unseen tree. In the second case the sky is dark, creating a feeling of night or stormy weather. In the third case the sunlit church becomes a feature area, and the attention is drawn to it almost exclusively by the manipulation of value.

Influencing viewers in this way has a long tradition. For over a thousand years, artists have repeated what may appear to be obvious, even funny, things. For example, pictures that have people walking into them or pointing into them were, and still are, common. You'll notice that you seldom see a boat sailing out of the edge of a picture. The car or carriage almost always rides into the picture. Birds fly in, and even weeds and branches will point to the subject. Used with discretion and taste, these kinds of tricks can be positive contributions.

One reason given for the dramatic turnaround in much painting beginning in the nineteenth century is that convention had reigned supreme

Roman courtyard, 1976. Brown felt pen.

for too long. Artists were so bound by convention that many felt they had lost their identity, independence, and freedom to create. This search for new ground shattered many illusions about art, and it continues today. However, even in the most controversial of art forms, an objective analysis will show that many, if not most, of the old conventions can still be found.

The principles of *rhythm* and *harmony*, for example, desirable characteristics of the finished sketch, are very often found in very abstract expressions. Rhythm is achieved by the recurring, regular cadence of similar objects or spaces in the field of the drawing. It follows the peaks and lulls of its closest relative, music. Harmony has to do with relatedness—relatedness in theme, in texture, and even in the psychological aspects of drawing. Harmony does not mean similarity.

No, that would be too pedestrian. But rather it refers to the analogous, the metaphorical, and the blending of associated forms, shades, and emotions into a unified whole. Conventions like rhythm and harmony are not to be taken lightly, and only the committed artist/designer can begin to manipulate such elements to his or her will.

Many factors are at work at once when you draw. Two of these factors might be simplified and called *surety* and *unsurety*. In other words, once you have committed yourself to a drawing, you are certain of some elements in it, whereas you are uncertain about others. You feel you can draw some parts, but not others. This is a critical crossroad for any drawing. What confounds most people is the seemingly logical conclusion that, since they can't draw some of the drawing, they shouldn't draw any of

Rembrandt. View Over the Amstel from the Ramparts, *c. 1647–50. Pen and wash in bister. (Courtesy of the Rosenwald Collection, National Gallery of Art, Washington, DC)*

Rome southward, 1975. Fine ball-point pen.

it. I have found this conclusion to be erroneous. Sometimes I draw what I can draw—grass, a shadow, a window—and even though I'm a bit apprehensive, the lawn, the light, and the building all follow in due course. Draw what you are sure of first. If this process seems appealing, then see what happens next. Break down complicated elements by drawing parts that you know you can do: ships at harbor, bridges, distant views. A drawing is a composite of many individual things, a collection as in a symphony, a museum, or a simple house, and somewhere one must begin to collect, arrange, and exhibit the interdependent aspects as a whole. When the parts support and reinforce the whole, the whole can sometimes be left to form itself.

Afterword

Out in the yard, 1982. Felt pen.

Giza, 1976. Drafting pen. (Courtesy of Dr. George Jones)

It is not easy to do independent work. Perhaps in some ways that is the central issue of education: placing a veneer of independence over one's associations with the world, sort of repetitiously putting schools out of business, answering enough questions but posing twice as many more, until *voila*—self-confidence, independence, and freedom from the system. You make it. You don't need it as much as it needs you. You are free to create.

There are abilities that prepare you for this freedom. The first is an ability to see. Drawing has a way of releasing the eye's otherwise detached associations with the world and freeing it to focus on the variety and beauty that is in all things. Second, you will achieve drawing freedom through technical abilities. This is the ability to manipulate the medium; it is a gift, through practice, that all art forms demand. Third is the ability to think. Personal confidence will free you to think creatively and realize the force of your potential. The ability to think will keep you open to the eye's search, to the exploration of the range of associations that constitute thoughtful ideas, to the maintenance of your identity through independence, and to a flexibility and willingness to respond to the endlessness before you.

Index